Fitzgerald's Mentors

Fitzgerald's Mentors

Edmund Wilson, H. L. Mencken, and Gerald Murphy

Ronald Berman

THE UNIVERSITY OF ALABAMA PRESS
Tuscaloosa

Manufactured in the United States of America

Typeface: Caslon

∞

The paper on which this book is printed meets the minimum requirements of American National Standard for Information Sciences—Permanence of Paper for Printed Library Materials, ANSI Z39.48-1984.

Library of Congress Cataloging-in-Publication Data

Berman, Ronald.
Fitzgerald's mentors : Edmund Wilson, H. L. Mencken, and Gerald Murphy / Ronald Berman.
p. cm.
Includes bibliographical references and index.
ISBN 978-0-8173-1761-4 (trade cloth : alk. paper) — ISBN 978-0-8173-5693-4 (electronic) 1. Fitzgerald, F. Scott (Francis Scott), 1896–1940—Knowledge. 2. Fitzgerald, F. Scott (Francis Scott), 1896–1940—Political and social views. 3. Fitzgerald, F. Scott (Francis Scott), 1896–1940—Friends and associates. 4. Wilson, Edmund, 1895–1972—Influence. 5. Mencken, H. L. (Henry Louis), 1880–1956—Influence. 6. Murphy, Gerald, 1888–1964—Influence. 7. Mentoring of authors—United States—History—20th century. 8. American literature—History and criticism. I. Title.
PS3511.I9Z55776 2012
813′.52—dc23

2011027756

Chapter 3 is a revised version of an essay that first appeared in *The F. Scott Fitzgerald Review* 7 (2009).

Cover: Gerald Murphy, Bibliothèque (Library). Courtesy of Yale University Art Gallery.

This book is dedicated to Barbara

Contents

Introduction

Teaching and Learning

F. Scott Fitzgerald's tutorial education began at Princeton with Edmund Wilson, continued in New York with H. L. Mencken, and began anew with Gerald Murphy in France. His friends left an archive of opinions about him: Mencken in his autobiography and reviews, Wilson in his essays and letters, Gerald (and Sara Murphy) in letters as well. Perhaps it should be said that they left a record of their own values that Fitzgerald did or did not live up to. That is nowhere better stated than in Wilson's essay "A Weekend at Ellerslie," a long look backward from the time of its writing (1952) to the time it describes (1928). Wilson's assessments often begin with a description of early experience followed by what might be called the years of evidence. The interval allows him to see how writers and others made their impression, then either vanished from or entered literary history. This particular essay is about artistic conscience, a subject more complex than it looks. It states, as scholars know, that Fitzgerald "had come to regard himself as somehow accountable to me for his literary career."[1] That needs to fit into a larger picture because accountability meant more than literary achievement.

In his essay on Christian Gauss, Wilson distinguished among various kinds of morality: "It was always Gauss's great advantage over the school of Babbitt and More that he understood the artist's morality as something that expressed itself in different terms than the churchgoer's or the citizen's morality; the fidelity to a kind of truth that is rendered by the discipline of aesthetic form, as distinct from that of the professional moralist: the explicit communication of a 'message.'"[2] Wilson's own mentorial relationships affected him deeply. He understood in theory that intellectual and moral issues diverged, but he sometimes failed the test of practice.

Fitzgerald had invited Wilson and other guests to Ellerslie, a property outside of Wilmington. The weekend began with a busy drinking night during which Fitzgerald became bored with the conversation and disappeared. He turned up later as a ghost with a sheet over his head and, one thing leading to another, set fire to Gilbert Seldes's bedroom. Wilson handled this admirably—the real damage was caused by social conscience. The essay's main point is Fitzgerald's hostility to Wilson and *The New Republic,* "the liberal weekly on which I was then working." Wilson gathered that he was not "on my side" of the Sacco and Vanzetti trial. He could not understand Scott's political indifference and admits it was one of the things that kept them apart. Wilson was offended especially by his "parody" of *TNR gravitas* in the letter of invitation to Ellerslie. The letter began by posing some urgent social problems in the form of mock editorials. One of them—it sounds very much like Shaw baiting Chesterton—remarked the glaring absence of the Fabian Society from the British General Staff. Not much of an infraction, but Wilson kept comedy at a safe and intellectual distance. He allowed himself to think that Scott's political attitude was itself a breach of conscience. The essay ends with a wonderfully modulated insult, recalling "the literary life of a period in which nonsense and inspiration, reckless idealism and childish irresponsibility, were mingled in so queer a way." I think that means Edmund was inspired and idealistic while Scott was all the rest. We begin to see some differences in the idea of conscience. One notable point: Wilson dismissed the "parody" of authority although it governed his disguised appearances in Fitzgerald's work.[3]

Fitzgerald was at the receiving end of quite a lot of advice about the written word. Some of that advice was given by Ernest Hemingway, Gilbert Seldes, and Max Perkins. Much of what they had to say was accurate and helpful. Does that fit our category? According to the *Oxford English Dictionary,* mentoring is the transmission of advice and guidance through teaching. But not everyone who advises fits the category. The process, I think, has to be identifiable, a record of statement and response. Mentorship has to take place consistently and over a measurable period. It may well deal with moral as well as textual matters but needs a conclusion; some specific idea has to find its correlative. In short, it takes place over time, has an object, and requires substantiation. The *Oxford English Dictionary* records, however, that mentors themselves may well turn out to be "irrepressibly assertive." That was the way Wilson saw himself, liable, he says, "to the assertion of moral authority."[4]

Fitzgerald often rejected guidance. It was not entirely a matter of his seeing the light then improving his writing by becoming more disciplined and well read. When Bernice in "Bernice Bobs Her Hair" abandons her soggy adolescent novels we think that she, like Fitzgerald, has moved on to higher things. But Fitzgerald's characters take a next step after abandoning the past: they show up the failings of improvement. It might be said that they detect its motivations.

Necessarily, that means they show up the failings of their mentors. That seems to be something we can take for granted, but I will at a later point suggest that there is more to it. Contemporaries—among them Wittgenstein—were engaged by the complexities of learning. The process is rarely direct and involves compromises. It is bound to cause misunderstandings. As Freud saw it, the teaching of morals creates (and may even proceed from) hostility. Virtue was repressive. Wilson's rationalistic theory was that he had changed his mind for the better when mentored, so there was no reason why Fitzgerald should not do the same. That implied a range of causes from his sheer inability to think—Wilson's first choice—to recalcitrance. Driven by this logic, Wilson took one of literary history's great pratfalls. In March 1922, he cited Edna St. Vincent Millay's remark that Fitzgerald was like a stupid old woman unable to describe the diamond she has been lent.[5] It was a parable of talent unequal to inspiration. In June 1922, Fitzgerald published "The Diamond as Big as the Ritz," a story full of insights into the habits of unjust power. It satirizes more than money—at the center is Braddock Washington's domineering rationalism. He has the wrong answer to everything human. We might want to give additional weight to a line at the end when John T. Ungar tells the ethically challenged Kismine, "you will grow old" admitting to "incredulous" listeners that you made the wrong choice between diamonds and rhinestones.[6]

Wilson gave Fitzgerald many ideas about education to adopt, modify, or eventually reject. He wrote often about his literary education, as in the essay on Alfred Rolfe, his teacher at The Hill School. The narrative moves from early times to his current state of mind and his relationships. The piece appeared between the death of Fitzgerald and publication of *The Crack-Up*. It establishes professional criteria, making it difficult to think of Wilson as a kind of gentleman of letters.[7] Here he asserts that literary criticism can only follow from training in languages. From the beginning, it must be comparative. It must be current. On those grounds alone he was never able to understand Fitzgerald's willed ignorance of French language and culture while he was in France. Writing demanded both a historical and a critical context. In his own case, after the Greek language came the recognition "that there was something worth having there behind the numbered paragraphs and paradigms."[8] Literature began with Homer, made its more or less orderly progress through time with each subsequent text having the kind of continuity established by T. S. Eliot. In fact, Eliot's view of the classics was at the heart of Wilson's criticism. Later, in *Upstate,* Wilson explained the failure of Van Wyck Brooks to grasp the conception:

> In endeavoring to acquaint himself with the whole of American literature, he had no time to catch up with the classics. Somewhere he refers to "the classics," meaning the Greeks and Latin writers, as if they all embodied the same ideals instead of representing a great variety of personalities and schools and periods; as if they stood as a solid refutation to the achievements of our own times . . . he talks as if the greatest writers were invariably "voices of the people" and gives a list that begins with Tennyson and Hugo and ends with Manzoni and Björnson. Brooks is childish about "form" and "content." He said to me once angrily at Wellfleet, when I questioned his theory of Eliot's evil influence, that Eliot was the person directly responsible for . . . misleading the young.[9]

The dispute mattered to Fitzgerald who used Eliot in his greatest novel; and very nearly made *Trimalchio* a household word. He understood Wilson's literary history and also the difficulty of using it directly in his own work. Just as Fitzgerald was thinking about the problem, Santayana wrote that he, too, "should like, therefore, to turn to the ancients and breathe again a clear atmosphere of frankness and honour; but in the present business [American culture in 1923] they are not very helpful."[10]

Allusion in Fitzgerald implies a Wilsonian grasp of literary history—and also our loss of the great tradition. Amory Blaine invokes Heraclitus and Monsignor Darcy reads the *Agamemnon.* The mention of both is wistful, as if they should matter more than they now do. Fitzgerald tells Max Perkins that he will prepare for his third novel by rereading the classics; and indeed there is Homer in *Gatsby.* But the difference is everything. Mencken had asserted that the ideal novel should be heroic, about a man consciously opposing tragic fate. In *Gatsby,* tragedy takes a different form, its effect depending on the distance between act and meaning. Do serious books now matter in the marketplace? Not according to Pat Hobby, who seems to have been reading the letters of F. Scott Fitzgerald: "authors get a tough break out here. . . . They never ought to come. . . . They don't want authors. They want writers—like me."[11] Fitzgerald's literary history is ironic: the Philippe stories are set in the heroic ninth century, although heroes exist only in the movies. Language itself becomes part of the joke. Philippe's dialogues—"Get back, you dogs! . . . Stand by, my men!"—await reincarnation by Hollywood hacks.[12] In fact, lines like, "Answer me like that once more, and I'll let daylight through you" will be heard in Pat Hobby's studio: "'You try to move me,' said the extra, lifting the hilt of his scabbard above the level of the table, 'and I'll hang this on your ear.'"[13] History repeats itself as farce.

Sometimes the distance contracts: the power of *Gatsby*'s ending comes from Milton and Marvell. And the graves at Shiloh are less forgotten because of Henry Marston in "The Swimmers," Sally Carrol Happer in "The Ice Palace," and Amory Blaine at the end of *This Side of Paradise.* Princeton is nowhere more compelling in Fitzgerald than when Amory envisions "the spirit of the past brooding over a new generation."[14]

Wilson's essay on Rolfe states that the aim of critical writing is mastery of a context—he chose for himself the New England beginnings of American literature. Fitzgerald developed his own context based on a romantic view of the American South. The Rolfe essay caused Wilson to think about the way we learn, and who we learn from. He modified his own sense of literary history because it had become clear that "journalism" provides freedom from the academy. He argued that the marketplace allows access to modernity—in his case, one had to pick up contemporary writers outside of class and against the institutional will. That is not an unfamiliar idea for scholars, but when Wilson defends it we can see that Fitzgerald also had an end in view. The way we learn to read and write was on Wilson's mind in the Rolfe essay, in his essay on Ben Jonson as both genius and pedant, and in his letters to and journals about Fitzgerald. Here is Mr. Rolfe's psychology of learning: "Greek wouldn't teach itself. He did not depend for this purpose on the natural rectitude of our inclinations—either his own or ours—any more than he did on the evangelistic Christ who was supposed to come to your rescue and give you a bracer of salvation."[15] The allusion is more than figurative: Wilson (like Fitzgerald) had secular evangelists to learn from. Both were citizens of a world in which sacral meanings were residually attached to life and art. Wilson is explicit on the connection between text, learning, and duty. I don't mean that art became for him what is conventionally thought to be an alternative religion. Without harshing the gig, that is what patrons of art believe, not artists. Wilson had the attitude of Eliot (and also of Dewey, James, and Santayana) who presumed that art was not only a high calling subject to conscience but also an access to reality.

Important passages in Fitzgerald and Wilson look back to what made them: learning and teaching. Wilson says of his essay on Christian Gauss, "it indicates to some extent the point of view from which I started off in my criticism of the twenties."[16] That is not the only reference to himself, because, like Hemingway and Gerald Murphy, Wilson thought about the impermanent arts, among which were his own: "I include such reminiscences of the classroom in the hope that they may be of interest in putting on record Gauss's methods as a teacher, for the work of a great teacher who is not, as Gauss was not, a great writer is almost as likely to be irrecoverable as the work of a great actor."[17] The journals and essays keep coming back to the inherent limits of mind and the endings of literary movements and reputations.[18] Wilson refers to teaching as if it might moderate these things. He was not so much alone as we might think: he belonged to his educational past, to what he called the "movement" of modern writing, and to political liberalism. When he talks about beliefs he invokes their sustaining institutions. Fitzgerald really was alone and had to develop oppositional ideas—there is more to "egotism" than self-regarding style or psychological attitude.[19] It connotes hard-won independence and, as Walter Lippmann noted, was a necessary reaction to false public consciousness. Lippmann did not believe in received wisdom. Wilson tends to put himself into an intellectual sequence, as in these lines from the Gauss essay: "the ripples [of influence] he started in motion were multiplied again and again."[20] Fitzgerald respected such pietàs and acknowledged influences upon him. He also sensed that at some level the obligation was honorific. His difficulties were more complex than those attributed to alcoholism or illness. He came into conflict with precisely those institutions important to his mentor.

The Rolfe essay and other Wilson pieces praise methodology and context. Writing begins with the correct use of language, then proceeds to the "control" of material. The theme recurs in the entire Wilson-Fitzgerald correspondence: Wilson's praise of *The Vegetable* was accompanied by the reminder that "you have a much better grasp on your subject than you usually have—you know what end and point you are working for, as isn't always the case with you."[21] Throughout Fitzgerald's work we see echoes of Wilson. Characters in his stories discuss the rights, habits, and nature of the very rich; the nature of democracy in America; the place of the past in our national life; the distinctions of social class; the illusory nature of ideals; and the never-ending dream of American progress. They are familiar with contemporary arguments about the Younger Generation, North against South, provinces versus Metropolis, the social role of women—and those books that really do need to be read at Princeton. Wilson gave him information and method but Fitzgerald, like Wittgenstein in 1929, understood that "no one can think a thought for me." Fitzgerald was not alone in thinking about the intellectual mandates of the Jazz Age:

> You cannot lead people to what is good; you can only lead them to some place or other. . . . I recently said to Arvid, after I had been watching a very old film with him in the cinema: A modern film is to an old one as a present-day motor car is to one built 25 years ago. The impression it makes is just as ridiculous and clumsy and the way film-making has improved is comparable to the sort of technical improvements we see in cars. It is not to be compared with the improvement—if it's all right to call it that—of an artistic style. It must be much the same with modern dance music too. A jazz dance, like a film, must be something that can be improved.[22]

We want to remember Wittgenstein's experience as a teacher and also his familiarity with the new arts. He understands that the purpose or at least the destiny of teaching is to be left behind. There is an enormously powerful passage following this citation about the way that "earlier culture"—which is always the property of the one who teaches—becomes forgotten. I think that Fitzgerald was on this side of the argument.

Wilson's articles and reviews certainly provided material for Fitzgerald's handling of public issues. They were programmatic: Wilson wrote to Lionel Trilling that being an editor at *The New Republic* from 1925 to 1931 allowed him to order "all the articles on cultural subjects in the back of the magazine" and to write whatever he chose in addition. Like Shaw, he managed "to impose . . . his values as an artist *and citizen*" on a great many people by his choice of coverage.[23] Before that, at *Vanity Fair,* Wilson had begun his long sequence of essays on American writers. While critics of the 1920s were dealing with topics like the unruly young or the unholy rich he wrote influential pieces on modern writers. But we don't go to *The Shores of Light* and *The Twenties* to recover his criticism of Sherwood Anderson. Wilson had a parallel life centered on the understanding of problems adumbrated by Dewey, Freud, Santayana, and Whitehead. Here he is on the train going back from California after trying to get Chaplin to do a movie on the nerve-wracking life of industrialism: "I read as much as I could understand . . . of A. N. Whitehead's *Concept of Nature*. . . . I was never at home with metaphysics, but I . . . accepted as plausible Whitehead's explanation of the world."[24] Wilson was in a sense overcome by the idea of relativity—it became an essential part of his understanding of Proust. He put a great deal of thought into the problem of perception, and even more into the larger problem of expressing that in language. When Fitzgerald describes a scene and also *the difficulties of understanding it* he shows his own formidable grasp of the philosophy of experience—and also what he has come to understand from Wilson.[25] He also shows the mechanics of transmission. It is worth pondering the sequence Whitehead-Gauss-Wilson-Fitzgerald: "I remember his later quoting with approval A. N. Whitehead's statement, in *Science and the Modern World*, that, 'when you are criticizing the philosophy of an epoch,' you should 'not chiefly direct your attention to those intellectual positions which its exponents find it necessary explicitly to defend. There will be some fundamental assumptions which adherents of all the various systems within the epoch unconsciously presuppose. Such assumptions appear so obvious that people do not know what they are assuming because no other way of putting things has ever occurred to them.'"[26] In his earlier novels—for example, Anthony Patch's bumbling about with "philosophy" in *The Beautiful and Damned*—Fitzgerald tried to name the process, to look at it from the outside. By the time of *The Great Gatsby*, he was able to show the process through character and dialogue. He was indebted to Wilson for his entry into the intellectual world, although that came at a certain cost.

During Fitzgerald's New York years he and H. L. Mencken wrote to each other; they also had conversations at lunch or while drinking infamous Coffin Varnish cocktails that were Mencken's personal defiance of Prohibition. They commented on each other in reviews, letters to their other friends, and in small, scattered memoirs. Mencken published the revised "Babes in the Woods" in *The Smart Set* (1919) and the landmark story "The Diamond as Big as the Ritz" (1922) after it had been turned down by the *Saturday Evening Post.* Mencken reviewed *This Side of Paradise* (1920), *The Beautiful and Damned* (1922), *Tales of the Jazz Age* (1922), and *The Great Gatsby* (1925).[27] He patiently responded to Fitzgerald's indefatigable literary, editorial, and dramatic projects. Fitzgerald knew Mencken first through his reputation, then through his work. A number of Mencken's essays published before the 1920s were assembled in the extraordinarily influential *Prejudices: Second Series.* Mencken thought it important to mention in his autobiography that this collection had been read by Aldous Huxley and reviewed by Fitzgerald.[28]

Fitzgerald's opinions of Mencken were balanced by those of Edmund Wilson—it would not be too much to say that there was a triangular relationship. I doubt that we can get at Fitzgerald-Mencken without going through Wilson-Mencken. Wilson admired *The American Language* and maintained a correspondence with H. L. Mencken for many years.[29] He thought highly of Mencken's literary knowledge, less of his critical principles. Wilson's many essays—"H. L. Mencken" (1921), "The All-Star Literary Vaudeville" (1926), "Mencken's Democratic Man" (1926), "The Critic Who Does Not Exist" (1928), "The Nietzschean Line" (1930), "Talking United States" (1936)—conclude that Mencken was accurate about something important to both of them, the stifling effect of public morality on writers. "Thoughts on Being Bibliographed" (1943) has more to add, bringing together Fitzgerald, Mencken, and Wilson himself. It widens the argument. First, Fitzgerald, who clearly did have some sort of epic grandeur: "I remember Scott Fitzgerald's saying to me, not long after we had got out of college: 'I want to be one of the greatest writers who have ever lived, don't you?' I had not myself quite entertained this fantasy because I had been reading Plato and Dante. Scott had been reading Booth Tarkington, Compton Mackenzie, H. G. Wells and Swinburne, but when he later got to better writers, his standards and his achievement went sharply up, and he would always have pitted himself against the best in his own line that he knew."[30] Thinking about Scott returns Wilson to the subject of teaching, a main connection to his intellectual life. He associates teaching with impermanence, beginning at this point in the essay to write about Mencken, whose fate foreshadows Fitzgerald's and his own. The project he is working on, collecting Mencken's letters, suddenly becomes "an ominous sign that the movement was folding back on itself before having finished its work."[31] The fear of impermanence is also built in to his Christian Gauss essay. Gauss had left little behind in the way of office occupied or policy fulfilled or work published. There was only his "influence" that mattered—but it was limited to "those who felt it."[32] As Wilson saw it, *learning* was marked by obligation and loss while *teaching* deferred one's intellectual disappearance.[33] Both contributed to one's sense of belonging to a tradition. Fitzgerald sympathized, but aggressively defended marketplace values. His essays and letters are about a career as well as a tradition.

Wilson published his first major essay on Mencken in 1921. Before it appeared, Fitzgerald wrote a letter to HLM about the connection between the three of them: "I'm deep in a new novel at present. Edmund Wilson John Bishop + all my friends and I are eagerly awaiting Prejudices 2nd Series, even tho we've read most of the essays Wilson, by the way, is doing an essay on you—not a mere blurb or puff but an analysis of your methods for the January or February Vanity Fair We were both talking the other night about how hard it is not to imitate your style at times."[34] In fact, their responses were more complex: Wilson respected Mencken as a guide to language and "common life" but distrusted his political philosophy. He thought that Fitzgerald did not really understand Mencken's essential point that common life is seen through common speech: "We have a genuine artist and man of first-rate education and intelligence who is thoroughly familiar with, even thoroughly saturated with, the common life. The rule has been heretofore for men of superior intelligence, like Henry Adams and Henry James, to shrink so far from the common life that, in a country where there was practically nothing else, they had almost no material to work on. . . . He is saturated with the thought and aspect of modern commercial America. . . . He has studied the habits and ideas and language of the common run of his countrymen with a close first-hand observation."[35] Mencken's "methods" noted by Fitzgerald and the "first-hand observation" noted by Wilson shaped their own understanding of the 1920s.[36] For one thing, *The American Language* (1919–36) had provided evidence that sales talk, magazines, ads, and "movies and talkies" affected usage even more than education did. But that is only part of Mencken's insight: "it seems to me that there is also something more, and something deeper. The American people . . . have shown an increasing inclination to throw off their old subservience to English precept and example."[37] That begins with but accounts for more than usage.

Wilson accepted Mencken's claim that colloquial speech adequately expressed human "hopes and aspirations." He argued that literature of the 1920s would develop not from high culture but from colloquial grammar and syntax:

> Looking back today, we can see that this first edition of *The American Language* marked a stage in the development of our literature. It marked the moment when the living tide of American had mounted so high along the sands of "cor-

> rect English" that some formal recognition was necessary. Six years later, in 1925, the review *American Speech* was started, and Sir William Craigie, one of the compilers of the big Oxford dictionary, sailed for the United States to begin work on a dictionary of American. . . . We must give Mencken credit for one of the really valuable services performed in our own day by American criticism for American writing.[38]

How was the transfer from speech to literature accomplished? The sense of self, according to Mencken, comes from the language describing it: "the American vulgate exhibits forms which plainly show that it is the spirit of the language to regard *self,* not as an adjective, which it is historically, but as a noun."[39] That is a revolutionary statement, and his list of examples is a tour de force. By the time we have gone through Mencken on reflexive pronouns ("He done it *hisself.* . . . Let every man save their *own* self") we realize not only that the concept of "self" is embedded in our usage but that it also means awareness, valuation—and intense self-regard.[40] Donald Davidson has written that *self* "depends on the realization of the existence of others, a realization that comes into its own with communication."[41] That is a good part of the business of the novel—as well as balancing, leveraging, and asserting the value of one self over another.

Wilson's review of *The American Language* cites Mencken's connection of words and "aspirations." These combine in Fitzgerald, as when Edith Bradin in "May Day" plans ahead for the mating dance at Delmonico's: "She would talk the language she had talked for many years." It is comprised of "current expressions, bits of journalese and college slang strung together into an intrinsic whole." It is a sign of the character she creates by using that language.[42] In his Mencken review, Wilson advises Fitzgerald among others to be more precise, and to use the new colloquial "vocabulary of literature."[43] Such advice came after the accomplishment.

Here is Myrtle Wilson's own language of aspiration and subjectivity: "I want to get one of those dogs . . . I want to get . . . I'd like to get . . . I don't suppose . . . I think it's cute . . . I'm going to have . . . I got to call up . . . I had a woman up here last week . . . I told that boy about the ice . . . You have to keep after them all the time. . . . The only *crazy* I was was when I married him. I knew right away I made a mistake."[44]

Mencken influenced the language of the novel, but Fitzgerald thought that he "made many mistakes" about other particulars.[45] One of those mistakes was his rejection of modernism; a second was his skewed idea of democracy in America: "What Mencken felt the absence of, what he wanted, and justly, back in 1920, got away from him, got twisted in his hand. Not because the 'literary revolution' went beyond him but because his idea had always been ethical rather than aesthetic. In the history of culture no pure aesthetic idea has ever served as an offensive weapon."[46] From the beginning, Edmund Wilson had warned that Mencken's theory of American culture was wrong. It is of course a moral pleasure to read about the mindless booboisie being mindlessly optimistic about mindless prosperity. But what if Mencken had given the new generation of writers an unreliable view of American class character? Fitzgerald knew from experience *how* Americans acted as they did; and he could see that Mencken explained *why* they acted as they did. But there was no correlation between what he lived and what he learned. During the early 1920s, Mencken kept telling him how to write about social reality, and Fitzgerald kept eluding him. The evidence is in those novels and stories in which Mencken's ideas reappear as comedy.

Mencken began to write about human motivation before the Great War and continued until the 1940s. One of his early statements, "The Advent of Psychoanalysis" (1918) lists works of "Freud and his friends." Mencken singled out *Totem and Taboo* and *Leonardo Da Vinci,* and the work of Jung, Adler, and their explicators. Like

Edmund Wilson and Walter Lippmann, he understood what the new psychology meant for writers: "Here, indeed, is a literature of singular interest. There is in it all the horror of theology and all the fascination of fiction." And—although his heart belonged to Havelock Ellis—he went considerably beyond sexuality: "this, indeed, is the crux of the matter: that ideas are determined, not alone by conscious causation, but even more importantly by unconscious causation—that the mental life of every one of us is partly the logical product of our environment, and partly a reaction from the natural desires which that environment opposes. Some of the most powerful of those opposed desires, particulary [*sic*] when they seem to be most thoroughly obliterated, are of a sexual character. . . . But, as Adler and Jung have shown, there are other desires in us that are powerful too . . . opposed implacably by the discipline that is civilization."[47] Given this insight—not much different from the thinking of Walter Lippmann and Edmund Wilson—what went wrong with his understanding of human motivation?

Mencken's lifelong obsession was human nature under democracy. In one form or another his essays and reviews are invested in the subject. But he took from history what Ezra Pound took from economics, confirmation rather than proof. His American history begins in the early nineteenth century with the Plantocracy. The old South, he imagined, had created the highest form of American civilization. It was—unlike New England—devoted not only to high culture but also to the conversation and style that made daily life interesting, as ideas cannot. Because it was secular, it was tolerant; because it was aristocratic, it never had to rely on the formlessness of political choice.[48] Mencken believed that the old South had been lost from within to yokel fundamentalism—"it has fallen to the bombastic trivialities of the camp-meeting and the chautauqua."[49] To explain the reversal he turned to the weakest and least developed of the new disciplines, crowd psychology. He thought of the electorate as simply a mob: in the South, rubes under the power of sermons and Sunday schools; in the North, Babbitts manipulated by journalism. He had a special animus against the literati—as did Santayana and others concerned with education. The defining historical event for Mencken was the First World War, not in Europe, but at home:

> All of us belong to crowds of one sort or another, and all of us, on occasion, think as crowd men, which is to say, emotionally, orgiastically, idiotically. The late war offered examples innumerable, and on a colossal scale. For a year or two the whole American people constituted a gigantic lynching party, and the most elemental reason was adjourned. It was physically dangerous, in those days, for an American to show any sign that he retained his good sense. Not only did the nether mob take to the highway, but also the corps of pedagogues aforesaid, and all the leaders in politics, and the massed clergy, and even the literati. It will be a curious enterprise, in the years to come, to study the phenomena thus unveiled.[50]

Mencken and other dissenters were treated that way during the war. But could that experience become a historical thesis? Fitzgerald did not think so, stating that while Mencken and Nathan were splendid advocates for literature, "the very first-rate writers" doubted *both* their literary and political-cultural ideas.[51] Wilson took sociology seriously and decided that middle-class complexities had simply eluded Mencken.

In the early 1920s, Fitzgerald used (and also parodied) Mencken on our democratic failures. The famous essay on "Professor Veblen" from *Prejudices: First Series* had in 1919 elaborated "our lack of an intellectual aristocracy." It asserted that "every other civilized country has such an aristocracy," which was "the natural corrective of enthusiasms from below."[52] Mencken's 1917 essay, "The Sahara of the Bozart," made the same points. In more polished form, *Prejudices:*

Second Series developed opposing views of aristocracy and democracy, centering on the quality of civilized life. It states that there was once an "art of living" so that life "got beyond and above the state of a mere infliction and became an exhilarating experience." We notice that Ardita in "The Offshore Pirate" despises the inherent "bleakness of living" and insists on the "value of life and the worth of transient things." Mencken praises "aristocratic manner," and Curtis Carlyle dreams of "an aristocracy" of style.[53] Mencken praises mind refracted in hospitality, leisure, and "the vague thing that we call culture"; while Anthony Patch in *The Beautiful and Damned* states that "Aristocracy's only an admission that certain traits which we call fine—courage and honor and beauty and all that sort of thing—can best be developed in a favorable environment, where you don't have the warpings of ignorance and necessity."[54] He means democracy.

That long-awaited piece on Mencken by Edmund Wilson appeared in 1921 while Fitzgerald was "deep in a new novel."[55] Wilson had much to say about the "philosophy" that was, I think, on Anthony's mind. Mencken's hatred of democracy had become cranky: "things are getting more and more democratic and consequently worse and worse. What we need is an enlightened aristocracy to take charge of society. But there has never been any such aristocracy and we are certainly not going to produce one. In the meantime, one can but curse the mob and die at one's post." Wilson thought that Mencken's political imagination had dwindled into mere sensibility, asking only "why should he take part in the brawl? What has he to do with the mob except to be diverted by its idiocy?" His tactic was to retreat into the self so that things move "without touching him particularly." One had to avoid "the rhapsodies of his disciples"—which both he and Fitzgerald accomplished.[56] Anthony Patch is by no means a version of Mencken but he does look like someone who has been reading too much of him.[57]

Fitzgerald learned from Edmund Wilson and H. L. Mencken that they expected him to think as they did, to follow their modes of writing. Even more, they expected him to follow their advice when judging contemporary literary ideas and reputations. But Fitzgerald was never going to be a son of Ben or a Sinclair Lewis. That is one reason why, in 1924, Fitzgerald wrote that he and Zelda had moved from New York to Paris "with a true conviction that we had left our old selves behind forever."[58] I don't think he means his own character *ab origine* or his jazz life in New York. He refers to the domination over him of other minds. In 1925, he began a memorable letter to Max Perkins on *The Great Gatsby* and his new intellectual independence:

> Dear Max:
>
> Under separate cover I'm sending you my third novel:
>
> *The Great Gatsby*
>
> (I think that at last I've done something really my own), but how good "my own" is remains to be seen.[59]

The terms he uses remind us that the search for an achieved self is one of the great themes in his fiction and in his frequent summaries of the state of his intellectual life. That search took a very different form under the influence of Sara and Gerald Murphy.

In France, the Murphys gave him access to the visual arts. There are essentially three versions of Gerald and Sara Murphy. The first recognizes Gerald's "cultural interests" and Sara's hospitality. Gerald himself was (relatively) rich, had great charm, was widely read, and was an unusually loyal friend to writers and painters.[60] According to this view, the "taste" and "style" of the Murphys were the virtues of patrons. Such a view misses an important distinction made by George Santayana, that "a criterion of taste" has in fact "a social career; it hopes to educate and to judge."[61] Gerald kept that criterion in mind and was notoriously a mentor to his friends. The second version was created by Fitzgerald in *Tender Is the Night* and by Hemingway in his recollections: the Murphys were dangerously rich; more notable for their existential freedom than for what they accomplished.[62] As to the third version, current work in the visual arts makes the case that Gerald Murphy was not only a subject of photography and painting but also a leading painter and intellectual of the 1920s.[63] The letters of both Gerald and Sara to Fitzgerald show that they influenced his thought. Wilson's anxieties about Fitzgerald's cultural indifference to France were premature: he absorbed modernism through Gerald and Sara Murphy from 1924 on.

The Murphys had been in Paris since 1921. Gerald worked with Fernand Léger, whom he called "an apostle, a mentor, a teacher."[64] He was photographed by Man Ray, which was in itself an accomplishment: "Man Ray met with a steady stream of aspiring and arrived literary lights seeking portraits in a modern idiom. Gertrude Stein let it be known that he was the only photographer in Paris allowed to make her portrait. . . . As Sylvia Beach put it, 'To be done by Man Ray meant that you rated as somebody.'"[65] Judging from the number of portraits done of Gerald, Sara, and their children and Man Ray's place in their lives, Sylvia Beach was an accurate witness.[66] Of course, medium and intention matter as much as occasion. I am thinking less of documentation than of Man Ray's conscious attempt to combine "art and daily life" in his work.[67]

Sara and Gerald were not shaped wholly by modernism in Paris. Both were born in the 1880s and belonged to the generation addressed by Mencken, Van Wyck Brooks, and, as noted, George Santayana. Here is what Santayana had to say about those who lived through the genteel tradition: "There are always private gentlemen whom the clergy and the professors cannot deceive. . . . But these clever people are not organised, they are not always given to writing, nor speculative enough to make a system out of their convictions . . . [and they cannot find in America] the open way to nature and truth." When they do look for it, they are baffled by functionaries.[68] The Murphys took art classes, started their own collections, visited the Armory Show of 1913, and knew patrons of the arts. Sara was herself a competent student of impressionism. F. O Matthiessen caught their moment when he wrote about Santayana: The choice for Americans was "to make art an adornment rather than an organic expression of life, to confuse it with politeness and delicacy."[69] In studying the Murphys we run up against many allusions to that "organic" art. They are in Dos Passos, Fitzgerald, MacLeish, and Man Ray. A workable conception of the Murphys begins with what they did not do: remain genteel patrons; join societies that "appreciated" the arts; remain silent about that matter of nature and truth.[70] They might have stayed to be cared for by servants in a small house near a fashionable square.

The Santayana essay of 1920 clarifies why artists would in 1921 want to leave America for Europe. In the three years before meeting Fitzgerald, the Murphys became assimilated into the life and work of modernism. In Paris, they worked on the scenery of the Ballets Russes, their first step past amateurism. Gerald especially took part in critical discussions with Picasso, Derain, and Diaghilev: "Scene painting brought the Murphys together with Picasso and enabled Gerald to blossom in an extraordinarily short time from an unfocused dilettante . . . into an accomplished artist with an eye-catching, hard-edged style that owed as much to poster artists like Cassandre as to Léger. Working for the theater inspired Gerald to monumentalize things: 'paint small objects on a scale considerably larger than life-size.' Goncharova had likewise left her mark on Gerald's vision, so had a new mentor, Léger, whose machine aesthetic became a principal guiding light."[71] Gerald began to paint in the cubist style; his work was exhibited at the 1923 Salon des Indépendants and the 1925 L'art d'aujourd'hui. Deborah Rothschild notes that 1923 was especially productive because of new theatrical commissions like his collaboration with Cole Porter in Rolf de Maré's ballet *Within the Quota.* The life of modernism was part of style. John Richardson describes the party given by the Murphys that year on a rented barge in the Seine: "In the annals of social history, the Murphys' party rates almost as high as the Rousseau banquet in 1908. Stravinsky switched the place cards; Goncharova read palms; Marcelle Meyer played Scarlatti; and, as usual, Cocteau tried to steal the show."[72] Reversals and masking might have been pure Dada; they also imposed a new sense of form on a new subject.

The Murphys moved to Antibes that year, with Gerald's major works yet to come: the iconic *Villa America* sign (1924–25) was done along with *Razor* (1924) and *Watch* (1925); then there were *Library* (1926–27), *Cocktail* (1927), and *Wasp and Pear* (1929) that affected MacLeish so deeply. Gerald's work continued, covering the same productive years as Hemingway and Fitzgerald while he saw them. That might be the point to look at. We know a good deal about the circumstances of life at Villa America and Paris but should also concentrate on subjects and techniques. Linda Patterson Miller has identified some of them:

> As Murphy sought to "*re*-present" real objects in his art, he had to discover these objects by stripping them bare, sometimes probing their interiors and placing them in new and unexpected relationships to their surroundings and to themselves. He brought this same process of discovery and enlightenment to his relationships, which explains his magnetic appeal to the other artists of his day. John Dos Passos admired the "mathematical elegance" of Gerald's mind and the "uncommitted freshness" of his vision, and he acknowledged that Murphy helped him to *re*-see ordinary objects and scenes, such that the streets of Paris became transformed as Dos Passos walked them with Gerald (which he did often

> during the 1920s). Gerald gave to his friends a "freshly invented world," said Dos Passos.[73]

The passage (like many others describing Murphy) centers on teaching. It follows the transference from an "ordinary" perception to its intellectual development. The language refers to ideas circulating at the time—even to certain texts stating them. Dos Passos, his wife Katy, and Archibald MacLeish mention Gerald's powers of vision but were, I think, focused on his powers of discovery—originality was the awareness of something already there.[74] That is more allusive than we may think. Sessions at Villa America and in Paris occurred after the appearance of *The Waste Land* and Eliot's essays on Donne, Henry King, and Marvell. To see ordinary subjects in a new way after 1921 is to reformulate both Eliot and Coleridge on "the sense of novelty and freshness with old and familiar objects." Eliot stated that seeing new meanings in commonplace images indicated more than perception: it was the result of a "firm grasp of human experience,"[75] MacLeish was devoted to (and imitated) Eliot; Fitzgerald used Eliot more than once in *The Great Gatsby;* and the title of Gerald Murphy's biography comes out of George Herbert. The phrase "new and unexpected relationships . . . to themselves" repeats definitions of metaphysical wit; the term "freshness" duplicates its use in the Marvell essay.[76] These allusions—especially to the value of "experience"—lead us to conceptions of intellectual life *within* domestic life.

Tender Is the Night is intuitive about the Murphys, factual about some details of their daily life. Our sense of their reality comes from additional sources. Gerald and Sara kept up a correspondence with Fitzgerald, Hemingway, and others. Gerald kept a notebook. Amanda Vaill's biography *Everybody Was So Young* and Deborah Rothschild's *Making It New* are repositories of facts about Antibes and also the other venues of their lives. Gerald's paintings are in themselves historical evidence—Picasso said they represented American culture of the 1920s. Some of Picasso's work of the 1920s was done at Antibes, imaging both Sara and Gerald. He describes the objects, colors, and designs he saw at Villa America, especially at La Garoupe beach. *The Pipes of Pan* shows Gerald Murphy while *Reclining Nude with Pearl Necklace* depicts Sara. There is a sizable body of documentary photographs by Man Ray. Gerald was painted by Fernand Léger; Sara was the subject of poems by MacLeish and Richard Myers; and both inform a number of memoirs of the 1920s.

However, even documentary evidence in the visual arts is ambiguous. Gerald's paintings of industrial and natural objects may be "coded," having a "private meaning" revealed by "hidden symbols" and forms under stress.[77] Man Ray's photos seem to be devoted to the accurate depiction of subject and moment, —while his films of the mid-1920s "allude to a graver disquiet than anything produced before. They also, interestingly, refer to vacation time near the sea, a special charmed existence on the beach—perhaps inspired by the seaside life on the Riviera, which Man Ray shared with Picasso, Hemingway, the Murphys, and his surrealist friends."[78] John Richardson and Deborah Rothschild discern in *The Pipes of Pan* indications of "troubled" psychology.[79]

We gather from the sources available that Gerald and Sara Murphy discussed with Fitzgerald the style of daily life, the nature of perception and the uses of technique in professional life, and their sense of human "value." Did their daily life at Villa America, as is so often claimed, constitute a form of art? It is difficult to argue with Picasso, Léger, and others who produced meaningful work about that life. Its activities, celebrations, and rituals became subjects of art so that the premise does seem to have been proved. How did that life affect Fitzgerald? He came to France after years of enduring Mencken's theory of aristocracy. Mencken was not interested in aristocratic politics; in fact, Walter Lippmann, Burton

Rascoe, and others ridiculed him because he never accounted for privileged injustice. Mencken was, however, a tireless defender of the existential virtues—ease, tolerance, and pleasure—associated with aristocratic style. If Fitzgerald was interested in those things conceptually in *The Beautiful and Damned,* this was a chance to see them in action.

In the studio, Gerald worked often with industrial objects under magnification. He imitated (and may have used) photographic enlargement. Many of his works depict things bought and sold. His perception of detail has drawn comparison between the visual and verbal arts:

> In Gerald Murphy's painting *Watch,* all the senses are brought into play. Florent Fels, who saw it in the *Salon des Indépendants* of 1925, found it at first "astonishing" and "soon seducing." But before the eye's seduction by the fourteen shades of gray in the painting, the ear responds to the ticking of this instrument of precision . . . [and is reminded of lines by] Jules Laforgue . . . the rich colors that lie hidden or subdued in *Watch* are brought forward [in *Wasp and Pear*] to astonish us with their richness, for here it is the wealth of the world that is on display. But we soon realize that the triumph of color is illusory, for it is projected so richly only so that the defeat that awaits it may be all the more clearly emphasized. . . . The pear's luscious female contour is echoed in that of what appears to be a mandolin standing beside it—so that everything that is desirable and lovely in life, all that can be touched, felt, and tasted, and all that can be praised in song, will soon be destroyed. . . . [It is] a visual version of William Blake's "The Sick Rose."[80]

If those paintings do contain such meanings, they must have had some bearing on what Gerald thought and what he discussed with

Fitzgerald. If the meanings were self-evident, then they were visibly at hand.

We've known for some time where to look in Fitzgerald for Sara and Gerald Murphy: as models for characters in *Tender Is the Night.* But if they are present in one work they are liable to be present in others. And they will be there in more than one way. Enough of their dialogue with Fitzgerald survives to indicate that he used their language of human relationship. The correspondence that began in 1925 does have recurrent themes—from the very first letter of that year Gerald refers to the subject of human "value" in a way indicating its familiarity as a subject of discussion between himself and Scott. In later letters to Fitzgerald (and also to Dos Passos and Hemingway) Gerald outlined his position on quite a bit more than personal style. Sara's letters to Fitzgerald are analytically impressive: "I should love to see Zelda too—I think of her face so often, & so wish it had been *drawn* (not painted, drawn). It is rather like a young Indian's face, except for the smouldering eyes. At night, I remember, if she was excited, they turned black—& impenetrable—but always full of impatience—at *something*—, the world I think. She wasn't of it anyhow—not really. I loved her. & felt a sympathetic vibration to her violence. But she *wasn't throttled,* —you mustn't ever think she was except by herself—She had an inward life & feelings that I don't suppose anyone ever touched—not even you."[81] I think that Fitzgerald's work opens up as a result of knowing Sara and Gerald, and that their existential awareness is duplicated when his own characters think about themselves in relation to others. So the case is not only that Gerald "had come to dictate my relations with other people" but that his ideas and Sara's—necessarily, I think—became part of the work.[82]

Those ideas were treated critically by Fitzgerald. That lifelong conversation beginning at Princeton with Wilson, involving Mencken and later both Sara and Gerald Murphy, occurred as major works by Freud like *The Ego and the Id* were being published. In that book all our social motives are probed, and mentors especially are held to account. There are correspondences between Fitzgerald's ideas and contemporary philosophy and psychology. Local discussions between Fitzgerald and his mentors reflected worldwide discussions about ideas. In regard to Freud, who has been studied to great purpose by scholars of *Tender Is the Night,* I have concentrated not on his clinical work but on his cultural reflections.[83] In the first third of the century he published works that covered conscience, friendship, and the process of mentoring. He revealed great sympathy for the ego, which is always in conflict with the (equivocal) authority of those who represent civilization. We tend to be anxious, even apologetic about Fitzgerald's egotism, but Freud frequently justified the urgent assertion of the independent self against what it had to learn.[84]

Edmund Wilson continued to see the issues in terms of education. In 1953 he wrote to Lionel Trilling about his Fitzgerald essay in *The Liberal Imagination.* That essay was about Fitzgerald's success as a writer. But Wilson offered an explanation for Fitzgerald's failure as a writer: "The trouble about Scott's case, when one begins talking about Goethe, etc., is that he didn't, in the third-rate Catholic school he went to, get enough of the right kind of education to sustain him in his absolutely first-rate ambitions." He emphasized that Scott had never *unlearned* his attraction to "the plutocratic society of St. Paul and Chicago."[85] In fact, *The Great Gatsby* keeps making Trilling's point that Fitzgerald's rich are deeply worth knowing because they are individuated. The argument was conducted in terms of probability on one side and politics on the other—it was as if Marx were criticizing Balzac. Wilson moralized the issue because he had no other position to take. In his mentorial way, Mencken wanted Fitzgerald to share his own profound distaste for democracy. Like Wilson, he believed that the fiction of success—Fitzgerald's métier—had no philosophical interest. That prevented him from understanding either *The Great Gatsby* or America after the Great War. Fitzgerald found his mentors often to be admirable, but that was no reason to believe them. His stories show the baffling connection between high-minded advice and real behavior. Social virtues cause endless comic reversals: Bernice and Basil Duke Lee try to become masters of their fate but always have to fight off lofty intentions. The stories are small fields of intellectual battle.

Scholarship has produced first-rate accounts of Fitzgerald's life and fiction, although there are still blank spaces on the map. I have tried in *Translating Modernism* and *The Great Gatsby and Fitzgerald's World of Ideas* to show his connection to minds outside of literature. Once we read Walter Lippmann, William James, George Santayana, and John Dewey we see how much Fitzgerald belonged to his times. Not to the 1920s that we so often imagine as an extended production of the Ziegfeld Follies but to one richer in ideas about art than any decade since. It remains to see how ideas actually reached Fitzgerald. He was careful to admit that he got many of them from his mentors. He also rejected many of them. Wilson et al. transmitted advice, censure, and argument, which produced resistance—one of the great patterns of Fitzgerald's work. "It's a good thing," Wittgenstein wrote in 1929, "I don't allow myself to be influenced!"[86]

1

Edmund Wilson's Authority

When F. Scott Fitzgerald '17 entered Princeton, Edmund Wilson '16 was already at the center of a group of writers who did lyrics for the Triangle Show, wrote humor for the *Tiger* and fiction for the *Lit* (*Nassau Literary Magazine*). In a sense, these were incidentals: he had already begun to rethink American literature and criticism. Wilson, John Peale Bishop, and Fitzgerald were enrolled at the same time in Christian Gauss's French tutorial group, which stretches the notion of serendipity. Lewis Dabney's life of Wilson recalls his authority even then: given Wilson's knowledge and Fitzgerald's enthusiasm, "they stepped easily into the roles of mentor and mentee."[1] That relationship was to last throughout Fitzgerald's life.[2]

Both men migrated to New York in the early 1920s, and in different ways they came to symbolize it. Wilson's letters identify Scott and Zelda Fitzgerald with the "jazz of American life" in New York City.[3] Fitzgerald's work depicts Wilson as its center of intellectual life. In "My Lost City" Fitzgerald describes his sighting of Wilson on the streets of New York, a place "entirely sufficient to him." Simply by observing him, Fitzgerald writes, "I got my first impression of that new thing—the Metropolitan spirit."[4] What did that knowledge entail, and how was it communicated? In a 1925 letter to Stanley Dell, Wilson remarked that he had no one to talk to at the highball hour: so "I have formed the habit of pouring it all into my correspondence to avoid the necessity of talking to myself."[5] Letters to Fitzgerald are set between those to his confidant Dell, and to Eliot, Mencken, Gauss, and others who made up the new cultural matrix. They show why Fitzgerald thought of Wilson as the incarnation of metropolitan learning. Lionel Trilling's essay on Wilson is essentially about New York's importance in his work: Wilson understood modern culture as it had been shaped by its setting.[6]

According to Trilling, Wilson's pieces in *The New Republic* (later collected in *The Shores of Light*) changed our minds about literary form and content, not to speak of its building materials. I think the Broadway pieces collected in *The American Earthquake* meet Trilling's standard.[7] One of the reasons why Nick, Gatsby, and Wolfshiem meet at Times Square is that American literature's GPS had shifted: both Wilson and Fitzgerald saw the life of Broadway as the key to "the life outside." Wilson's references to Broadway provided material for Fitzgerald and other writers:

> The new acts . . . fit into the Follies better: you have, in almost every case, a fast-moving dynamic act in place of a slow or vague one. Instead of Ring Lardner's rather casual Rip Van Winkle sketch, there is a terrific team of rube dancers, and Will Rogers with his halting drawl has been replaced by the machine-like energy of Eddie Cantor. Ann Pennington has also been added, so that, with Cantor and Gilda Gray, you have now perhaps the three highest-pressure performers in the city all on the same stage. The tempo of the show is now uniform, and it is the same as that of the life outside. This is New York in terms of entertainment—the expression of nervous intensity to the tune of harsh and complicated harmonies. When, afterwards, you take the subway home, it speeds you to your goal with a crash, like a fast song by Eddie Cantor; and in the roar of the nocturnal city, driven rhythmically

> for all its confusion, you can catch hoarse echoes of Gilda Gray and her incomparable *Come Along!*[8]

Names, ideas, and themes from Wilson reappeared in Dos Passos, Fitzgerald, and other writers.[9] For example, D. H. Lawrence described New York's "confusion that has no obvious rhythm" in his review of *Manhattan Transfer* (1925). Like Wilson, he concentrated on social effects, adding that there was a detectable "systole-diastole of success and failure" in New York lives.[10] Fitzgerald's description of Gatsby's second party reshapes Wilson's "complicated harmonies" into "many-keyed commotion." At the Plaza, the motif of "confusion" applies to Tom's mind in particular; then to Nick, Gatsby, Daisy, and Jordan with "the city lights behind" them. Even Wilson's subway is there, and the "tumult" that extends to everything around it.[11] Dissonance in Dos Passos and Fitzgerald follows Wilson's sense of "the bewildering confusion of the modern city." Such atmospheric nervousness is conveyed by intellectuals, and especially by Broadway comics like Joe Cook who show the way modern "minds are beginning to work." In 1924, Wilson described material that would be used by Fitzgerald in 1925, especially his thoughts on the incoherence of experience.[12] In the "F. Scott Fitzgerald" essay of 1922, Wilson called Fitzgerald the poet of "the Age of Confusion itself."[13]

The essays and letters consistently see writing in terms of Broadway genres and motifs: The "F. Scott Fitzgerald" piece of 1922 states that *The Beautiful and Damned* is a "farce" about "actors" in a "harlequinade." The last term is used also in "The Follies as an Institution" (1923) to describe Ziegfeld, daily life in New York—and Fitzgerald's novels.[14] A letter to John Peale Bishop (1924) describes Wilson's idea for "a great super-ballet of New York . . . a pantomime explained by movie captions and with a section of movie film in the middle" to be undertaken by Chaplin.[15] "The All-Star Literary Vaudeville" (1926) says that our great novelists have always been "one-man turns," so that current writers must likewise be performers on the public stage.[16] Wilson uses the idea of "vaudeville"—a favorite conception—as a metaphor of intellectual life. His "Broadway" review (1927) argues that current expressionist plays can't begin to approach "vulgar American life"—something better done by melodramas like *Broadway* and *The Shanghai Gesture.*[17]

Leon Edel outlined three great accomplishments of Wilson in the 1920s: he was the first to understand modernism, he recognized that "subjective modes" would dominate culture, and he was right about the replacement of naturalism by symbolism.[18] Broadway was essential to all three. Ruth Prigozy has shown that Broadway was not used by Fitzgerald as a backdrop to the fiction. Its numbers were used to define "personality, plot, and idea."[19] In addition to revues, shows, and variety there was a new contender: "In 1934, when asked by a newspaper to list his ten favorite plays—or outstanding impressions in the theater—Fitzgerald selected three from films: Charlie Chaplin in *The Pilgrim,* Greta Garbo 'in her first big role,' and 'David W. Griffith's face'" as he imagined it during the filming of *Birth of a Nation.*[20]

If Wilson represented the intellectual life of New York for Fitzgerald, Fitzgerald became an example of the city's sweet life for Wilson. Wilson's essay on the *Follies* says that it has "something of Riverside Drive, of the Plaza"—and also "of Scott Fitzgerald's novels."[21] He thought that Fitzgerald was one of the few writers to capture the vitality and also the moral dissonance of the city. That needs some detail, and theater history is more specific: in the "early twenties, vaudeville was often concerned with the culture that was replacing Victorianism: sensual, expressive, individualist." Burns and Allen were a lot less innocent in "Lamb Chops" of 1926 than they later became as icons of our own sentimentality. As a 1918 reviewer said of Sophie Tucker, she brought to the audience a reminder of "tottering monogamy"—just what did Mrs. Rip Van Winkle do "when her husband was asleep?"[22]

Wilson and Fitzgerald were both connected and separated by their ideas. Fitzgerald associated New York with more than dissonance. He saw in it the American rise to success, while Wilson saw American cultural failure. The introduction to *The Undertaker's Garland,* a collaborative effort of 1922, explained that John Peale Bishop and Wilson, recently returned from the war and with Paris on their minds, believed that "New York was no more fitted for love than it was designed for art. . . . Our cries 'for madder music and for stronger wine' met with absolutely no response, and we were informed that any attempt to get the latter would be considered a criminal offense. For money, it appeared, was the thing to get."[23] That doesn't sound promising for an author like Fitzgerald, who wrote narratives of success in his fiction and analyses of the literary marketplace in his letters.

In later life Wilson was acerbic, demanding, and overbearing. He wasn't built for human relationships—Mary McCarthy called him "The Minotaur," which seemed appropriate. When dealing with Fitzgerald he could be kind and charming—although Leon Edel observes that Scott knew even in the early 1920s he might be "seriously hurt" by disagreeing with him.[24] One of Wilson's letters of 1921 is endlessly patient, full of intelligent asides about the kind of reading Fitzgerald should do and the kind of criticism he should avoid. Wilson was right about most things: telling Fitzgerald that novelists like Cabell couldn't possibly last, reminding him that Mencken had his limits.[25] Letters to Stanley Dell, John Peale Bishop, and Fitzgerald are really introductions to a literature course that went on for a lifetime. The process, however, was adversarial. Fitzgerald thought of Wilson as his "intellectual conscience," but I think the phrase needs examining.[26] The connection of mind to conscience suggests useful knowledge conveyed through criticism. It also suggests willingness on one side and toleration on the other. Wilson did give Fitzgerald reading assignments, and he went over his writing. He coached mental discipline.

But that does not exhaust the meanings of "conscience," because those meanings changed during Fitzgerald's career. That was one result of the flow of analytical work by Freud. Translations of his work on the super-ego were publishing events, just as were new works of Eliot and Joyce. In *The Ego and the Id* (1923) Freud defined "conscience" as a form of emotional and intellectual constraint.[27] By 1930, the date of *Civilization and Its Discontents,* even "good" conscience was seen to be authority—not all of it legitimate—internalized. In fact, Freud was much concerned with its psychic costs. He uses literary terms to describe the process as he often does: the super-ego keeps "a watch over the actions and intentions of the ego . . . exercising a censorship."[28] The nineteenth century (at least until Nietzsche) had found conscience to be liberating, a means to become nobly selfless. After Freud, it was found to be inhibiting.

Wilson knew Freud thoroughly and often invoked him. Some of his great, lasting essays begin with a particular Freudian insight and then develop a view of authorial personality. His explanation of the work follows from his explanation of the writer's emotional condition. His method of revaluing Jonson, Dickens, and Kipling certainly ought to be applied to himself as well—not because it's rough justice, but because the presumption is that other writers understood his aims. The essay on Jonson begins with an allusion to Freud and other analysts; its subject is the relationship of the writer to an audience of friends and followers. Wilson is especially concerned with Jonson as a figure who needed to educate his readers. One aim was to have them recognize classical allusions, another was to recognize how well he had modernized the classics. Jonson, was, however, so immoderately ambitious that the second aim overwhelmed the first. There was a dysfunctional connection between the genius and the pedant. Teaching became a form of personal vindication, while the display of learning was an act of aggression, a challenge to his inferiors. The picture of Jonson that emerges from his plays—they deal largely with misanthropes—may be a seventeenth-century self-portrait. Wilson's description of Jonson may be a twentieth-century self-portrait. The literary works of both men are brilliant, entertaining, ebullient, while their shared personality remains emotionally distant, without empathy. Both resemble a comic stage figure: "an unsociable and embittered personage who sometimes represents virtue and censors the other characters."[29] Ultimately, knowledge becomes a weapon for both; as Wilson observes, Jonson defends his own work by criticizing other writers.

The Kipling essay also combines admiration for the work with unsparing analysis of its author. Parts of it—I am thinking of the passage in which he asks, "What became of this English Balzac? Why did the author of the brilliant short stories never develop into an important novelist?"—seem to bear on his own ambitions as well as on his sense of Fitzgerald.[30]

Wilson is incognito in Fitzgerald's stories, as in his own works about other writers. His presence can be felt when Fitzgerald's characters get conscientious advice, when they become self-aware, and when they are unwillingly educated. A great deal has been written about Fitzgerald's ego, but that should be viewed against his super-ego.

Wilson's conversations, letters, essays, and reviews criticize the novels and stories, with the first two of these also criticizing Fitzgerald's discipline and temperament.[31] Fitzgerald's letters and essays admit his debt to Wilson. They comment on books he has been made to read and critical standards he has learned to follow—or not. Then there is the oceanic content of Fitzgerald's fiction.[32] His reaction to mentoring may be seen when characters go through the tiresome experience of being improved. His artists, dancers, directors, musicians, and writers have to change standards in order to please a paying audience. Comic dialogues especially diminish big ideas, undermine their authority, show their temporality. "Contrary thoughts," according to a central study of Freud, "are always closely connected with each other and are often paired off."[33] The stories have many parodies of instruction, high and low.

In Fitzgerald, ideas are judged by experience. There are a number of contemporary texts on the subject, for example, George Santayana's famous essay on William James that makes the point that experience—the natural subject of literature—is empirical, deeply resistant to generalization: "The word experience is like a shrapnel shell, and bursts into a thousand meanings. . . . physics and mathematics seem to me to plunge far deeper than literary psychology into the groundwork of this world; but human experience is the stuff of literary psychology; we cannot reach the stuff of physics and mathematics except by arresting or even hypostatising some elements of appearance, and expanding them on an abstracted and hypothetical plane of their own. Experience, as memory and literature rehearse it, remains nearer to us than that."[34] Santayana emphasized the "passionate" immediacy of experience; Fitzgerald believed that literature mattered because of its emotional affect, its power to charm, persuade, and evoke. He argued against Wilson's rationalism until the end of his life. Points made around 1920 are restated in conversations with Sheilah Graham, in letters to his daughter, and by fictional characters who do not enjoy moral progress.

After the publication of *This Side of Paradise* (1920), Wilson pointed out that Amory Blaine (recognizably Fitzgerald himself) "is a fake of the first water" whose views on "art, politics, religion and society" are laughable. Wilson advised Fitzgerald to "read something other than contemporary British novelists: this history of a young man stuff has been run into the ground and has always seemed to me a bum art form, anyway."[35] Fitzgerald agreed, even lectured his friend Thomas Boyd on the subject in terms taken straight out of Wilson. But he also disagreed. Under the lash of instruction he admitted that "this writing of a young man's novel consists chiefly in dumping all your youthful adventures into the reader's lap with a profound air of importance."[36] Yet he never gave up on the genre.[37] We think of critical agreement or disagreement as final verdicts, although in the daily life of writing they take the form of ongoing conflicts. In Fitzgerald the same critical ideas can be asserted and also rejected. Contemporary works indicate that the process is not paradoxical. Here is Wittgenstein asking in "Following a Rule" whether we ever *really* "explain to the other person what you yourself understand?" Instruction is something of a psychological game in which "you get him to *guess* the essential thing." And of course it has all the makings of conflict, not to say of psychological disaster: "how do I know that it doesn't mislead me?" This matters a great deal because Wittgenstein's larger project was the stubbornly empirical interpretation of philosophy. The refractions of independence are authorial: "how can a rule shew me what I have to do at *this* point?"[38] Many of Fitzgerald's characters ask that question—before Bernice bobs her hair she asks the same thing.

In 1906, a publisher had requested Freud and other writers each to list ten "good" books for him. Freud replied that the formulation was unclear because stories might be "good" in different ways. As for himself he preferred not to invoke "magnificent works" of world literature. Instead, he chose "books which one has enjoyed oneself and gladly commends to others, but in connection with which the element of timid reverence, the feeling of one's own smallness in the face of their greatness, is not particularly prominent."[39] In short, it was the connection of the book to the ego that mattered more than its connection to cultural history. The issue was tested in an especially interesting way in 1918. A letter from John Peale Bishop to Fitzgerald made the same points as Freud—the occasion was actually that of commending a book to a friend. Bishop had in mind Compton Mackenzie's *Youth's Encounter*, the archetype of that "bum art form" loathed by Wilson:

> O God! O God! How wonderful *Youth's Encounter* is! Perhaps it meant more to me now than it would have done at Princeton, but it has done more than all the sociology in the world to make me feel life is worth living. I rose from its reading with that "free" feeling you have when the first thaw of spring takes the courses of winter. What if the light is too golden, the half-light too blue? Who would have them otherwise in a story of youth is an ass and the father of asininity. This is undoubtedly the true, the undefiled aim of the novel—to present—but how shall I venture to speak to your ears, so fearful of banalities?—any how it's not sociology. . . . Now to come to your own book. Scott, I think if you will recollect the volume above, or the account of Wells' youthful heroes, or Anatole France's *Le Livre de Mon Ami,* the glaring defect of your book will be noted. . . . Each scene—chapter what you will should be significant in the development either of the story or the hero's character.[40]

What a great letter this is! Bishop knows that Mackenzie's book is not "good"; he commends it to a friend who shares his cast of mind. He likes what he reads not because it reshapes the literature of the West but because it is an authentic "story of youth." Given what Freud has contributed to that concept, the letter opens up a great deal about the psychology of reading—and even more about conflict between the ego and literary conscience.

Another letter, from Fitzgerald to his daughter in 1940, has become famous for its explanation of romanticism. It is in itself a mentoring statement, explaining to Scottie (who is electing college courses) how the process works. Fitzgerald's example turns out to be John Peale Bishop on poetry while at Princeton: "It isn't something easy to get started on by yourself. You need, at the beginning, some enthusiast who also knows his way around." The next step is comparative reading, seeing "the difference between poetry and non-poetry"; that is, choosing between texts assigned or making "discoveries." Then, reading what you will "a hundred times." Ultimately one recognizes (especially in Keats) "a scale of workmanship" for modern writers.[41] Sheilah Graham's biography states that "we talked about my reaction to his work. I had judged it intellectually, not emotionally, he said."[42] Fitzgerald was a mentor with different aims than Wilson. He emphasizes "reaction" to reading, something that scholars have known for a long time. We might add, though, that his remarks are reconstructive; implying the rethinking and even reenactment of what he had experienced. I think his own tutorials with those he loved were meant to show how a critical education should be done.

A 1921 letter to a childhood friend, Robert D. Clark, says that "I've let myself be dominated by 'authorities' for too long—the headmaster of Newman, S.P.A, Princeton, my regiment, my business boss—who knew no more than me." Shortly after that he asked Wilson to give him "the kind of critisism [*sic*] I'd like more than anything else." He wanted copyediting: knowing when to "Cut . . . enlarge . . . Invert sentence."[43] When Amory Blaine tolerates a friend's "radicalism" at Princeton he finds that his opponents are not mindless administrators—"I mean they're the best-educated men in college—the editors of the papers." By the end of the story Amory understands that it might have been better to "have started all enquiries with himself. He was his own best example."[44] That sounds like romantic egoism, but it reflects some fairly considered judgments. Walter Lippmann's *Public Opinion* (1922) would soon conclude that unexamined social conscience does not explain anything. It may turn out to be one among many "artificial censorships." In order to reach valid conclusions, the world has to be individually "explored, reported, and imagined."[45]

Comic dialogues in Fitzgerald often allude to conscience, as when Mr. Rooney gives his favorite advice to Basil Duke Lee: "why don't you get wise to yourself?"[46] It's always possible that the advice comes from a deep well of altruism. It's also possible that certain Fitzgerald characters are entirely responsible for the social messes they create. But the reader of the 1920s understands the context—especially if he has been talking to Edmund Wilson or reading Walter Lippmann. There is a luminous passage in Lippmann about advice intended to indoctrinate. It states that social "harmony" may be "imposed" upon "the self-opinionated person," and Lippmann was as suspicious of that as Fitzgerald. In fact, he wrote that it was perfectly defensible to be "bored by these schemes of rights and duties."[47] We don't want to reduce Fitzgerald and his resistant characters to personality types, then to imagine that his stories proceed from their fallibility. Perhaps it should be put this way: they may be wrong (repeatedly, in the case of Basil Duke Lee) but they are doing the right thing by asserting their subjectivity. In Fitzgerald, social order itself is part of the problem. *Civilization and Its Discontents* makes the point that one doesn't have to do anything "bad" to feel guilty. In fact, "we notice how little" the accusation tells us because some outside authority has already decided for us "what is to be called good or bad." That authority never defines the problem. But it does make us feel anxiety, guilt, and even fear. The worst case is when some "stronger person" shows superiority, demands conformity, threatens punishment. That punishment arrives as the loss of their "love" or friendship.[48]

The namesake of "Bernice Bobs Her Hair" comes from the provinces. Her family has some money. She is sentimental but plain-dealing. Her more sophisticated cousin, Marjorie, thinks that the money part is fine although the rest is stylistically dated. As the story begins, Bernice overhears Marjorie's opinion of her unforgivable innocence and is induced to trade it in for popularity. She develops a "line" about being witty, brazen, and immoral but has to promise to get her hair bobbed (a daring and sexy venture in 1920) in order to make good on her claims. After Marjorie manipulates Bernice to do it her friends drop her—it's easier to give up friendship than challenge Marjorie. Given its lightness of being, the story has much to say about Bernice's life merging with a charged historical moment. The subject, however, is not entirely manners and mores.

Marjorie Harvey is a perfectly realized editorial figure. She is opposed to Bernice who is authorial, responsible not only for the idea of producing something—a new self—but inhabiting it. Marjorie knows far more than her provincial "mentee"; for example, that established texts like *Little Women* are as "out of style" as the Victorian virtues.[49] She understands or at least alludes to Freud but is a rationalist who believes that knowing something is as uncomplicated as being someone.[50] She tries to remodel her cousin through teaching. Wittgenstein (I don't think that his artillery is too big for this target) had some thoughts about the process of intellectual change. When the "pupil" is lectured by his mentor, unforeseen problems arise: one needs to detect in an (assigned) speech "the tone of voice, the play of expression, the genuineness or falsity of feeling, the intentions of the speaker."[51] That carries over into the relationship itself. In Wittgenstein, these things become part of the *problem* of mentorship. In this story mentorship appears to be disinterested. It looks like a *solution* to the small problems of social life. In fact it raises doubts—which become in Fitzgerald the true subjects of the story. I don't mean doubts about the moral effects of being disingenuous or the social penalties for getting your hair bobbed. The power of this story comes from its recognition of the "intentions" and character of the mentor. Bernice learns *from* Marjorie, but the more interesting part of the story is what she learns *about* Marjorie.

Bernice's real education begins when a conversation about strategy turns into a study of personality. Bernice knows that Marjorie is "cold" and does not like "sentiment." The description seems to go beyond reasonable detachment. Are her traits more important than her tactics? She is an emotional bully who uses her knowledge to intimidate and control. In fact, she does make Bernice feel "guilty." Marjorie's narcissism is conveyed when she refuses to answer Bernice, "but gazed pensively at her own image in the mirror."[52] The ancient literary device embodies self-absorption and implies destructiveness. Freud thought that self-love was aggressive, and he went to drama and the novel for examples: "Indeed, even great criminals and humorists, as they are represented in literature, compel our interest by the narcissistic consistency with which they manage to keep away from their ego anything that would diminish it."[53] Judging from this, Marjorie is willing to improve her cousin but needs also to dominate her. "Popularity" seems innocent enough and easily obtained. We forget the implication: it means what other people think of us. As the story proceeds we can see that it is a commodity inviting brokerage.

There are several kinds of "authorial intrusion" (xxiv) in the Basil stories. Basil and his friends read Alger, Tarkington, and Richard Harding Davis—while their author lives in the world of Joyce, Eliot, and D. H. Lawrence. Certain allusions like that about the "still unhatched eggs of the mid-twentieth century" in "The Scandal Detectives" (16) remind us of Fitzgerald's double viewpoint: he examines the prewar world by using ideas that came after it. Our own minds have literally enough been changed in the interval. There is an especially useful passage on that change in Wilson's imaginary dialogue of 1924 between Van Wyck Brooks and Fitzgerald. Here is "Brooks" ponderously to "Fitzgerald": "Freud has shown us that the things we say in jest are as significant as the things we say in earnest—they may, in fact, be more significant, because they reveal the thoughts that are really at the back of our minds and that we do not care to avow to the world."[54] Such thoughts need time to develop and language to express them. I think that Basil's comedy of growing up is connected to Fitzgerald's comedy of the repressed ego taking a late revenge on conscience. That is best stated at the end of "He Thinks He's Wonderful" when Basil realizes that his destiny is "not to forget, but to carry his wounds with him" (98).

In "The Perfect Life," Basil wants love, power, and approval. He has presidential daydreams and no morality to speak of. The following sounds like a reader who has had enough of Basil, which is easy to understand. He "only too often yields to the temptation to become sycophantic, opportunist and lying, like a politician who sees the truth but wants to keep his place in popular favour."[55] That actually is Freud describing the harassed ego in a world that never gives up bullying it. It is impossible to like Basil because he remains one of the great brats in American literature. Yet we don't want to judge either Basil or egotism too quickly because both reflect our world of bad conscience. Fitzgerald states that "the real restraining influence on him was fear—the fear of being disqualified from achievement and power" (125). Freud states that a main source of fear is conscience.

In this story Basil is recovering from a bad start at St. Regis School. If we remember the early stories of the sequence, he has been accused of being a coward, liar, and poseur—none of which is as aggravating as his enlarged sense of self-esteem. He is hated to the degree that he loves himself. However, in this story Basil regains popularity after playing well in a football game against Exeter. One consequence is that his classmates temporarily respect him; another is that John Granby, a St. Regis alumnus and genteel wowser, tries to recruit Basil for Princeton.[56] Granby is against alcohol. He is also against "other things"; that is, sexuality, and he views pantry raids of crackers and milk as crimes against property. He wants to have Basil go to Princeton where he can be mentored into good conscience; until then, he is to be an inspiration to the frosh at St. Regis, who are still blank slates of morality. Granby is by no means Edmund Wilson; but he does represent the will to fill other minds as if they were unoccupied spaces.

Basil may be modeling his "line" on Granby, who has discovered the right mix of intimacy and backslapping earnestness. But something more is going on. George Dorsey sees part of this when he explains Basil to his mother:

> "But I like him," George insisted, and then he added hesitantly: "It's just some funny way he's got to be lately."
>
> "How?"
>
> "Oh, just sort of queer."
>
> "But how, George? I don't want you to bring anyone into the house that's queer."
>
> "He isn't exactly queer. He just gets people aside and talks to them. Then he sort of smiles at them."
>
> Mrs. Dorsey was mystified. "Smiles at them?"
>
> "Yeah. He gets them off in a corner somewheres and talks to them as long as they can stand it, and then he smiles"—his even lips twisted into a peculiar grimace—"like that." (126–27)

Those smiles and grimaces ask for interpretation. George is mystified, but what he misses is later picked up by his sister, Jobena. What George sees is the denial of pleasure. What Jobena sees is its disguise. It takes her only a moment to deduce—and predict—what Basil wants: "he's a nasty little prig. . . . He gave me the old-fashioned moral lecture about nicotine and modern dancing and kissing, and about that upright, straightforward man that was going to come along some day—you know that upright straightforward man they're always talking about. I suppose he meant himself"

(136). Jobena has been around a lot of "oily and horrible" operators, which gives us some insight into the cultural moment. We can see why she might choose a hopeless drunk like Skiddy De Vinci, who at least is not a fraud. She won't have to put up with those "choice words, fascinating anecdotes, select sentiment, chaste point of view, and resolute piety" used by John Granby, Basil Duke Lee—and Elmer Gantry.[57]

There are two kinds of predicaments in the Basil stories. One is about bragging, looking good, being sufficiently annoying while staying ahead of parents, teachers, and the lynch mob in short pants. The other, as stated in "He Thinks He's Wonderful," is about the intellectual pleasure of controlling other people. In that story, Basil is permanently "under the impression that his advice had been asked" about the conduct of life (84). He is—of all things—a meddling little mentor who tries to remake Joe Gorman; then, in "The Perfect Life," Jobena Dorsey and himself. He fails miserably at each attempt to change minds, morals, or character. Fitzgerald understood his reputation as an "egoist." The ego, however, exists in relation to the super-ego, creator of good rules that are impossible to follow. That doesn't make Basil into Mickey Rooney, but it goes a long way toward understanding the resentment of learning.

The ego retells its story of conflict in unsuspected ways. In 1936, Gilbert Seldes wrote to Fitzgerald about his next novel and made some penetrating observations about his life, his work, and modernism. Sooner or later, he said, "you will have to say your complete say, not only in fiction, but in the facts about yourself and the part you played at the beginning and what you think of it now."[58] In order to cover the "facts" about himself Fitzgerald used different genres. He certainly tried conclusions: how many lines are there in his fiction asking "what was the implication" of experience? That is Basil Duke Lee thinking "of his own past" and being much less trivial than we expect (132). That moment of awareness anticipates the burden of self-interrogation in "Babylon Revisited" and other works. Seldes wanted what all critics want, orderly recollection and explanation of what writers know, how they come to know it, what their mutual relationships were. Fitzgerald did have his "say" about these things, but distributed "facts" about himself among stories, letters, and essays. According to Leon Edel, that was Edmund Wilson's practice as well: "we glimpse the 1920's," he says, "in phrases, bits of speech, miniature scenes."[59] Seldes asked for a memoir, while what we have are lines from many dialogues. Such reticence is familiar. Lyndall Gordon's biography cites Eliot's belief that *only* the work "will 'give the pattern . . . of the personal emotion, the personal drama and struggle, which no biography, however full and intimate, could give us.'" She adds that those elusive facts about private life are in "the morass of the manuscript."[60] Fitzgerald seems to have agreed: at the very beginning of his career, in "Head and Shoulders," a would-be author says that we all try "to express ourselves" but not always in a "written book"—in fact, consciousness contains all our "unwritten ones."[61]

2
H. L. Mencken's Democratic Narrative

In the sixth chapter of *The Sun Also Rises* (1926) Jake Barnes and Harvey Stone agree that Mencken is "through now." There are differing explanations for this. Mencken's biographers assert that his departure from the literary scene was voluntary: he had left *The Smart Set* in 1923 for the *American Mercury* to devote himself to the fabulous crankiness of our public mind. He preferred politics to literature, as did his magazine audience, so that the move was a good marketplace decision. I think that Hemingway implied his failure to persuade readers interested in *both* politics and literature.[1] Mencken's *Notes on Democracy,* which also appeared in 1926, was kindly but dismissively reviewed by Edmund Wilson, whose reasoning still holds true. Mencken's view of "the inferior man" in America was intellectually liberating. He had the right enemies: spineless politicians and a middle class with a mental metabolism "exactly comparable to what goes on in a barrel of cider."[2] But he thought in terms of groups, classes, and the eternal mob while modernists were subjective, uninterested in public life. In a letter of 1923, Fitzgerald stated that Mencken and George Jean Nathan "had a most stupendous and far-reaching influence on the whole course of American writing." However, "their influence was not so much on the very first-rate writers, though even there it was considerable, in many cases as on the cultural background."[3] As to that background, Wilson consistently found Mencken to be a better guide to language and to (some) literature than to politics.

It would be fair to say that Mencken disliked both modernism and modernity. He evaded Eliot, respected Joyce from a distance, had a low opinion of Hemingway—hence, the shot across his bow. Mencken attracts biographers, and one of his most sympathetic, Terry Teachout, defends his editorial policies at the *Mercury* in 1924. It was the first general magazine to cover jazz seriously; it tried to review dance and the visual arts; and it maintained some interest in literature. However, "modernism mainly went unremarked in its pages."[4] Mencken still mattered as a literary critic—but he still judged art for its formal clarity and moral intelligibility, unsure that now medium mattered as much as subject. He had been, however, a first-rate patron. Fitzgerald had this to say in 1923: "the vogue of books like mine depends almost entirely on the stupendous critical power at present wielded by H. L. Mencken. And it is his influence at second hand that is particularly important. Such men as Weaver in *The Brooklyn Eagle,* Bishop in *Vanity Fair,* Boyd in the *St. Paul News,* and dozens of others show the liberal tendencies which Mencken has popularized."[5] In short, Fitzgerald respected Mencken's editorial qualities, including those "liberal tendencies" for which he was then known; although today, given the positions he took on Franklin Roosevelt and the Second World War, the term "liberal" does not come easily to the lips.

One of Mencken's most admirable talents was encouraging writers on their own terms. He took risks like publishing Fitzgerald's early work in *The Smart Set.*[6] Looking backward, Scott wrote to Zelda in 1940 about editorial interference at the *Post:* "The man who runs the magazine now is an up and coming young Republican who gives not a damn about literature and who publishes almost nothing except escape stories about the brave frontiersmen, etc., or fishing, or football captains—nothing that would even faintly shock or disturb the reactionary bourgeois. Well, I simply can't do it. . . . An explanation of their new attitude is that you no longer have a chance of selling a story with an unhappy ending (in the old days many of mine *did* have unhappy endings—if you remember.)"[7]

Fitzgerald appreciated Mencken because he encouraged new authors and redefined the importance of contemporary fiction, replacing extinct species with writers such as Joseph Conrad. His discovery of Theodore Dreiser was part of a campaign to promote a writer's curriculum featuring the late work of Mark Twain as well as Conrad and H. G. Wells. Before these figures appeared on Fitzgerald's reading lists they were on Mencken's. Fitzgerald's letters and interviews acknowledge Mencken's effect on current writing, on his own writing, and on the rising tide of novelistic literacy he attributes to "the one man in America for whom I have a complete respect."[8] He got from Mencken not only a relative sense of importance of the work of Ibsen and Nietzsche but also the tactic of invoking their ideas among his own. He was not above using Mencken's essays on women, and he dug hard into the great vignettes of money, millionaires, and mobility in America.[9] There was always the work of rejection, vital for modern writers who had to change the tastes and buying habits of the national audience. Mencken looked more clearly than we do now at Edith Wharton, who sometimes "settled down into a valley of fustian"; he argued that "Howells . . . and the rest of that elder company have run their race."[10] He made room in the marketplace for writers like Fitzgerald.

When Fitzgerald and Wilson read "The Ashes of New England" in *Prejudices: Second Series,* their vocation would have been justified. In America, Mencken said, the pleasure of words must look like a seduction from the real business of life, an offense requiring apology to preachers and businessmen. Other pleasures were included: our peculiar institution in the North was, he thought, "Freudian suppression." That alone guaranteed him Edmund Wilson's support. He knew where civilization was located; and at least part of Wilson's vision of New York came from Mencken's prior discovery of Metropolis as a novelistic idea. It was a new venue for the mind, holding in one place "the whole, gross, glittering, incredibly stupendous drama of American life."[11] Mencken set up a grand opposition between those who thought American literature ended with the nineteenth century and those fascinated—as he was—with the reenactments of our national life in the movies and the Ziegfeld Follies. He believed also that "criticism of criticism" was academic, unhelpful to novelists.

Yet the relationship between writer and editor was ambiguous. Mencken's recollection of Fitzgerald in *My Life as Author and Editor* is an elegy to a wasted talent; Fitzgerald's praise of Mencken in the 1934 edition of *The Great Gatsby* adds that he was the man who "got off the train" when modern writing became modernism.[12] Fitzgerald's letters to Mencken praise him to his face, while his letters to other writers about him can be nervously apologetic. These are early fault lines: Mencken, like Edmund Wilson, has receded into the unread past. *The Great Gatsby* seems now to say considerably more about our lives and arrangements than all of their theories. That would have been unbelievable in 1925.

Mencken had an early intellectual impact. In his 1920 letter, Fitzgerald stated that he, Edmund Wilson, and John Peale Bishop were eagerly awaiting the publication of *Prejudices: Second Series* after having become "saturated with Menckenia."[13] Paul Elmer More was puzzled by the connection and asked, "why do [the young liberals] and a man like Mencken consort together so readily, when . . . they ought to be at one another's throats?"[14] Mencken offered a Unified Field Theory of literature and society—if one could but abandon one's self to it. It began with a plausible idea: because culture in the United States was genteel and sentimental, an obeisance to Puritanism, the purpose of writing was not "to interpret life, but to varnish, veil and perfume" it.[15] Here is Mencken's argument on America from the long-awaited *Prejudices: Second Series.* There is first the disease, then the cause, finally the condition:

> [Our literate are] Knights of Pythias, Presbyterians, standard model Ph.D.'s, readers of the *Saturday Evening Post,* admirers of Richard Harding Davis and O. Henry, devotees of Hamilton Wright Mabie's "white list" of books, members of the Y.M.C.A. or the Drama League, weepers at chatauquas, wearers of badges, 100 per cent. patriots, children of God.
>
> So far, the disease. As to the cause. . . . It is, in brief, a defect in the general culture of the country—one reflected, not only in the national literature, but also in the national political theory, the national attitude towards religion and morals, the national habit in all departments of thinking. It is the lack of a civilized aristocracy, secure in its position, animated by an intelligent curiosity, skeptical of all facile generalizations, superior to the sentimentality of the mob, and delighting in the battle of ideas for its own sake.
>
> What one beholds, sweeping the eye over the land, is a culture that, like the national literature, is in three layers—the plutocracy on top, a vast mass of undifferentiated human blanks at the bottom, and a forlorn *intelligentsia* gasping out a precarious life between.[16]

Edmund Wilson and Fitzgerald appreciated these sentiments, but both had their doubts. If we look at "May Day," done when Fitzgerald was intellectually reliant on Mencken, we can see the attractions of social theory. We can also see Fitzgerald's rejection of determinism. He understood that personality was too complex to be reduced to formal categories like aristocrats, boobs, and mob; he kept to his guns, arguing years later against preconceptions in the new medium of movie scripts.[17] He was concerned with phenomena within a textual or visual scene because perception affected character. He based his sense of self on romantic poetry—a genre nearly invisible to Mencken—that took for its subject our change from original innocence. He asserted the values of experience, convinced that individuals learned empirically. "May Day" is both a short story and a psychodrama showing conflict between author and editor.

Mencken accepted "May Day" for *The Smart Set,* where it appeared in July 1920. It is in some ways a remarkable piece, yet, as Matthew J. Bruccoli wrote, it may not be comprehensible on its own terms. The story is, he writes, a parody—"a burlesque almost, of another kind of writing"—and one needs to find out "how to read" it."[18] I think that Mencken recognized his own ideas in this story—they can be seen in "The National Letters" sequence in *Prejudices: Second Series.* Those essays cover the salient political points of the story, dividing the social world into components that were useful to Fitzgerald for a short time: artist, mob, and an insufferably material privileged class. We see them in the early stories and in *The Beautiful and Damned.*

"May Day" came out several months before *Prejudices: Second Series.* Yet in the letter of 1920 that I have cited, Fitzgerald assured Mencken that he and his friends had already "read most of the essays."[19] Mencken continuously revised—really cannibalized—his earlier work.[20] Bishop, Fitzgerald, and Wilson would have seen early versions of some of those essays in *The Smart Set* and the New York *Evening Mail.* There were even passages reborn from *Prejudices: First Series* of 1919. Mencken's ideas about America were incessantly restated for his annually increased audience.

The time and place of Fitzgerald's story are especially important because they were dictated by Mencken's historical chronology. Mencken thought that the Great War had reified the condition of American life: "a philosophy is not put to much of a test in ordinary times. . . . When it shows its inward metal is when the band begins to play. The turmoils of the late lamentable war, it seems to me, provided for such a trying out of fundamental ideas and attitudes upon a colossal scale." The treatment of dissent revealed that the people of the United States were really *divided* into plutocrats, intellectuals, and the mob. Fitzgerald's cast includes the patriotic mob driven by resentments, and a genteel, mindless, and materialistic ruling class that is perfectly able to do without intellectuals. Their role was to become apologists for "the mob run wild."[21] That left the "artist" or intellectual as our national consciousness. The central problem of this figure is "recognition" as a functional part of American society—"But the business is slow, uncertain, heart-breaking. It puts a burden upon the artist that ought not to be put upon him."[22] That is Mencken in late 1920; a *Smart Set* essay of 1919 had already established that in our America there is "no protection to an individual of assertive originality, and he is forced to go as a suppliant to a quarter in which nothing is his by right, but everything must go by favor."[23] Mencken's conclusion is that artists will neither get such recognition nor be able to succeed in the marketplace. There is no way out for an artist in America—or for poor Gordon Sterret, the victim not only of love but also of Mencken's dialectic.[24]

Here is a letter from Fitzgerald to Charles Scribner in 1920: "My new novel . . . concerns the life of one Anthony Patch. . . . He is one of those many with the tastes and weaknesses of an artist but with no actual creative inspiration."[25] Gordon Sterret himself says in "May Day," "I used to think I was clever, talented, an artist. Now I know I'm nothing."[26] We want to remember that the representative figure of the failed artist took Fitzgerald years to develop. It was indispensable not only to his fiction but also to his sense of self.[27] But we can see its connection to "The Lonesome Artist" theory in Mencken: "Thus falsely judged by standards that have no intelligible appositeness when applied to an artist, however accurately they may weigh a stockbroker or a Presbyterian elder, and forced to meet not only the hunkerous indifference of the dominant mob but also the bitter and disingenuous opposition of the classes to which he might look reasonably for understanding and support, the American author is forced into a sort of social and intellectual vacuum, and lives out his days, as Henry James said of Hawthorne, 'an alien everywhere, an aesthetic solitary.'"[28] Mencken's "The Intolerable Burden," explains why artist, mob, and plutocrat—the cast of "May Day"—are always in opposition: "It is lesser men that we chiefly have to deal with in this world, and it is among lesser men that the lack of a confident intellectual viewpoint in America . . . makes itself most evident."[29] Fitzgerald would have seen this in 1919, before it was reconstituted. He did more with this insight than its author, realizing that the artist's character mattered more than his condition. Weakness is the strength of this story.

"May Day" adopts Mencken's thesis that the Great War clarified our *domestic* condition.[30] It is divided into mob and plutocracy with an artist literally on the social perimeter. The first two groups have a conspiratorial connection—think of Peter Himmel agreeing with Carrol Key and Gus Rose: "That's what I say! Kill the Bolshevik! Exterminate 'em!" (319). Is that convincing, or does theory become unwieldy, separated from character as in the postwar cartoons of George Grosz? Dean and Himmel have to carry a lot of ideological weight. We know them by the things they buy—Dean especially has a strong symbolic connection to commodities, buying power, and money. Sometimes we see them as louts on Broadway—more often as illustrations of Mencken's plutocrats. The story keeps trying to bridge that difference, as in that moment of pure hatred when Dean tosses a five-dollar bill to Gordon who folds it carefully and puts it in his pocket. At a later point Himmel—bored, passive, drunk, useless—actually thinks about himself being "in a measure symbolic" (317).

Fitzgerald's mob looks very much like Mencken's. The "Cultural Background" essay in *Prejudices: Second Series* invokes "some extra-eloquent Red" on the city streets who needs badly to be beaten.[31] Fitzgerald provides the "little Jew with long black whiskers, who was waving his arms and delivering an excited but succinct harangue. . . .—'What have you got outa the war?' he was crying fiercely. 'Look arounja, look arounja!'" He is in fact beaten in this doctrinaire part of the story. Readers might like to see more of his dialogue because of its practiced rhythms and coldly intelligent allusions. However, the Jew does not show up again—nor does the mental energy of his delivery. He has been given a malicious tone that indicates a reserve of character: "Are you rich? Have you got a lot of money offered you?—no; you're lucky if you're alive and got both your legs; you're lucky if you came back an' find your wife ain't gone off with some other fella that had the money to buy himself out of the war! That's when you're lucky!" (305). There is no response because in Mencken the mob has a voice but not a mind.

Key and Rose categorically have "the very lowest form of intelligence" and not a great deal of "consciousness" (304–5). Those are ascribed: mob mentality, an obsessive Mencken topic, is discussed in *Prejudices: Second Series* and the rearranged pieces that make up *Notes on Democracy* (dating as far back as 1913). Mass man does not have the capacity of self-awareness. In Fitzgerald, although they have important ideas, the members of the mob have nothing to say. And why should they? *Notes on Democracy* asks: "What does the mob think? It thinks, obviously, what its individual members think. And what is that? It is, in brief, what somewhat sharp-nosed and unpleasant children think. The mob, being composed, in the overwhelming main, of men and women who have not got beyond the ideas and emotions of childhood, hovers, in mental age, around the time of puberty." Mencken concluded from early (and I think primitive) studies in behaviorism that mobs accurately showed life without "mental processes."[32] The idea of a mob was central to his notion of Americans full of morbid social anxieties but unable to state them.

Fitzgerald's characters, who are unpredictable, find themselves locked into Mencken's social world. That world, as Edmund Wilson put it when reviewing *Notes on Democracy,* is just as abstract and even "imaginary" as the terrain of any novel. Wilson writes that in actual life what Mencken takes for opposites in national character often merge, become "transformed into one another."[33] In his "Imaginary Dialogues" Wilson invents a moment of debate between Van Wyck Brooks, who disapproves of writing for money, and Fitzgerald, who reminds him that there is "creative" pleasure in making—and spending—it.[34] So far as both Wilson and Fitzgerald could see, Mencken's categories are impermanent. In "May Day" they dissolve.

"Consciousness" is an issue in this story because Fitzgerald's characters don't have any *internal* connection to Mencken's ideas about life in America. This beginning work has a powerful and accomplished understanding of the mind's variousness. To some extent, every novelist lives in the intellectual world of William James: nothing is more common in America than "the conversion of ourselves" to something different: "*a man has as many social selves as there are individuals who recognize him* and carry an image of him in their mind."[35] Fitzgerald understands irrationality, mercurial change, and absolute self-absorption. From page to page his characters are contradictory—in one scene of "May Day," Edith has five different views of what she will do about Gordon although none of them have anything to do with his success or suitability. How important is this view of character? In his review of *Notes on Democracy,* Wilson stated that Mencken's conception of bourgeois character "has not been equaled by any other recent literary creation, *with the possible exception of Scott Fitzgerald's flapper.*"[36] Conflict was unavoidable between the two convictions: one assuming that character was static, predictable, and socially determined; the other that it was governed—as Edith Bradin realizes—by "the twist of her imagination" (312). Or, to take Ardita in "The Offshore Pirate," "all the men and women she had known were but driftwood on the ripples of her temperament" (272).

Mencken's definition of the novel was a record of life conducted under the influence of ideals, opinions, and morals while subject to "laws, institutions, superstitions, traditions and customs." His preferred version of fiction showed "some one man's struggle with his fate" set within a reasonable account of the forces affecting him.[37] He wanted high seriousness and found that in the work of Dreiser who had shown individuals as members of groups and natural laws behind human motives. Dreiser's *Jennie Gerhardt*—for Mencken the peak of our national novel—"depicts the life we Americans are living with extreme accuracy and criticises that life."[38] Mencken did not have much to say about the operation of the mind, although we know that he accepted Freud's theory of the unconscious, and he appreciated the play of psychology in novelistic character. It took some daring for Fitzgerald to assert his own critical values. "May Day" is built around the character and mind of a social class known to him and dismissed by his mentor. One reasonable question is whether their trivial lives deliver as much insight as the moral largeness demanded by Mencken.

The narrator tells us about Key and Rose; the *gratin* tells us about themselves. Lionel Trilling remarked on the argument about the very rich between Fitzgerald and Hemingway, "the truth is that after a certain point quantity of money does indeed change into quality of personality: in an important sense the very rich *are* different from us. . . . Fitzgerald was right, and almost for that remark alone he must surely have been received in Balzac's bosom in the heaven of novelists."[39] The rich in this story are Mencken's plutocrats. Fitzgerald places them in exemplary situations in which money, class, and style are the evident issues. But the difference is everything. When we see the young and rich in this story thinking about themselves, they are more complex, and they carry more psychological weight than either Mencken or the *Saturday Evening Post* wanted. Even Peter Himmel, farther down than he imagines on the Chain of Being, works out the "permeating symbolism" of his moment (317). But nothing is more symbolic than the fact that these characters can't stop thinking about themselves. Mencken's problem is to display plutocracy; Fitzgerald's is to show how minds work.

Edith Bradin is both self-aware and authorial. These passages tell us what she knows about herself and show the extent to which her mind is focused on Fitzgerald's problems of creating a narrative:

> She thought of her own appearance. Her bare arms and shoulders were powdered to a creamy white. She knew they looked very soft and would gleam like milk against the black backs that were to silhouette them tonight . . . her reddish mass of hair was piled and crushed and creased to an arrogant marvel of mobile curves. Her lips were finely made of deep carmine; the irises of her eyes were delicate, breakable blue, like china eyes. She was a complete, infinitely delicate, quite perfect thing of beauty.
>
> She thought of what she would say to-night at this revel, faintly prestiged [*sic*] already by the sounds of high and low laughter and slippered footsteps, and movements of couples up and down the stairs. She would talk the language she had talked for many years—her line—made up of the current expressions, bits of journalese and college slang strung together into an intrinsic whole, careless, faintly provocative, delicately sentimental. (311–12)

"May Day" has begun with the great divide in American "consciousness" and "intelligence." Mencken believes that the "artist" alone is capable of useful introspection, but this story complicates the issue. It turns out that the self is just as much created as it is ascribed, that the "artist" does not have a monopoly on awareness, and that this particular story insists on refracting issues of authorship. Fitzgerald is dealing with models of character adapted from Mencken—while having them express the details of his own enterprise. Edith does this on a very high level. Is she right about self-creation? In "Experience, Nature, and Art" (1929) John Dewey took up the same point, insisting that it was wrong to say that "such arts as music, poetry, painting have characters unshared with any natural things whatsoever." In fact, enhanced sensual enjoyment is generally desired and has a lot to do "with other activities and products."[40] What a light this casts over the opposition between Mencken and Fitzgerald, and on the effort made by Jay Gatsby (and Daisy Buchanan who is good at it) to create reality around them. I've mentioned that it might have seemed impossible in 1925 to think of Fitzgerald being a better guide to reality than Mencken. My sense of it, though, is that *The Great Gatsby* is more sociologically and imaginatively accurate than Mencken's view of American life. Fitzgerald was able to establish a view of change and response to experience. It was based on the view of James and Dewey that personality was fluid.

The dance differs from its imagined form. Edith's dates turn up like (and resemble) clockwork. In a long cinematic scene they move one by one into the range of her perception. They are seen—as a lens sees subjects—in terms of assorted artifacts and body parts: a moustache, a fair-skinned man, someone who once played the ukulele, a fat man, even Philip Dean in minimalist form as "a man with prominent teeth" (313). That is what Dean becomes in the rest of the story; it is his great distinction. Are these *only* twists of her imagination or approximations of the way the mind actually works? Edith imagines herself as Aphrodite; decides to marry Gordon and cure his weakness; is disgusted by his appearance; pities him; finds him ridiculous, revolting, and boring; discovers that she does not really like weakness at all. We are prepared to understand that there are few correlations. It doesn't matter what the facts are. The ending of "May Day" is not random because Fitzgerald ran out of inventions. He needed to choose between Mencken's view of predetermined social types and his own idea of ungovernable change and complication in human character. By making the right choice, he made it possible for the Muse of Tragedy to show up at Delmonico's.

Matthew J. Bruccoli's *Some Sort of Epic Grandeur* mentions that Mencken probably influenced "Fitzgerald's attempt to write a deterministic novel."[41] Fitzgerald inherited from Mencken not only that fleeting purpose but also other ideas about the novel. And some of them needed to be refuted before he could find his way as a writer. For example, Mencken despised one particular story often retold in America, the narrative of success. He saw it restated in all of our forms of public opinion. It was the burden of advertisements,magazines, movies, sermons—and midcult literature. What did that narrative state? That bourgeois life was about getting somewhere without thinking about the cost of the experience or its consequences. Its grand circumstance was making money out of making widgets. It was literature for the material life, just a shade away from propaganda. What did it ignore? Questioning fate, arguing motives, finding ambiguities of character. What did it never dream of? Imposing form significant enough to tell a story. Two things will strike us almost immediately about this view. The first is that Mencken sounds right. The second is that he's missing something. Just a few years before, Freud had written about the literature of success. He knew that it could be perfectly meaningless in terms of style; from the start he admitted that he did *not* read "the writers most highly esteemed by the critics, but the less pretentious authors of novels, romances and short stories, who nevertheless have the widest and most eager circle of readers of both sexes."[42] His review established the centrality of the author in the tale, showing how life's circumstances, as in a case history, are rewritten. "Success" stories were not simply about democratic-industrial working life but about the psychological trauma of thinking about it. After all, such a theme involved judgment of the self—and it told us a great deal about the writer of the tale. But Mencken did not want to look deeply into the subject. He dismissed the democratic narrative as an attempt by yahoo culture to praise itself:

> To get on: this is the aim. . . . I describe the optimistic, the inspirational, the Authors' League, the popular magazine, the peculiarly American school. In character creation its masterpiece is the advertising agent who . . . marries the daughter of his boss, and so ends as an eminent man. . . . false drama, Sunday-school drama, puerile and disgusting drama. It . . . awakens a response only in men who are essentially unimaginative, timorous and degraded—in brief, in democrats, bagmen, yahoos. The man of reflective habit cannot conceivably take any passionate interest in the conflicts it deals with.[43]

Nothing from Mencken to Dwight MacDonald could be more plausible and, I think, more inviting to intellectuals. Yet Freud had recognized the inner importance of such fiction, reminding us that so-called success stories were at least as much about the intelligentsia who produced them as they were about the bourgeoisie who inhabited them:

> The creative writer does the same as the child at play. He creates a world of phantasy which he takes very seriously. . . . As people grow up, then, they cease to play, and they seem to give up the yield of pleasure which they gained from playing. But whoever understands the human mind knows that hardly anything is harder for a man than to give up a pleasure which he has once experienced. . . . Let us take the case of a poor orphan boy to whom you have given the address

> of some employer where he may perhaps find a job. On his way there he may indulge in a day-dream appropriate to the situation from which it arises. . . . He is given a job, finds favour with his new employer, makes himself indispensable in the business, is taken into his employer's family, marries the charming young daughter of the house, and then himself becomes a director of the business, first as his employer's partner and then as his successor. In this phantasy, the dreamer has regained what he possessed in his happy childhood . . . Our dreams at night are nothing else than phantasies like these.[44]

In the summer of 1921, Fitzgerald wrote to Edmund Wilson that "culture follows money."[45] (The letter angrily referred to the relationship of America and Europe as if Rome were displacing Greece.) Fitzgerald's phrase denotes that political power and economic power shape the subjects of art. It connotes that they also shape our attitudes about art. The importance of the phrase lies in Fitzgerald's reversal of the idealistic assumption that money should follow culture. His statement means that the values of the marketplace are legitimate subjects of the novel. They may not be moral or beautiful but they are the conditions of industrial-democratic social life. The narrative of success became his métier. Over the next few years, Fitzgerald made a considerable investment in that narrative. After Mencken had faintly praised *The Great Gatsby*, Fitzgerald sent him a letter that needs every now and then to be read over: while there may have been faults in the novel, he wrote, there was "not a frailty in the theme."[46] The theme of success in a material world, despised by Mencken, became in Fitzgerald (as in Freud) a convincing democratic narrative. Its great advantage turned out to be factual because it demonstrated that advertisements, magazines, and movies had become part of "culture." And even in popcult there were ironies too hard to bear.

Mencken had a philosophy but needed a history. In search of chronological proof, he argued that America once did have a caste sympathetic to the patronage and practice of the arts. His famous essay "The Sahara of the Bozart" satirized the politics, religion, and writing of the New South—and it identified in the Old South an actual civilization higher than our own. The essay (it was in that volume of *Prejudices* awaited by John Peale Bishop, Fitzgerald, and Edmund Wilson) identified the aristocracy of the Old South as our great source of post-Enlightenment toleration for the works of the mind. Certain of his points were to echo in F. Scott Fitzgerald's mind and show themselves in unexpected places.

The following is an account of Mencken's idealized and probably invented Plantocracy.

> Indeed, there was an elegiac quality to the sections of the "Sahara" in which Mencken wrote of the Old South. He celebrated a lost race, a once-civilized land "with men of delicate fancy, urbane instinct and aristocratic manner—in brief, superior men. . . . It was there, above all," he continued, "that some attention was given to the art of living. . . . A certain noble spaciousness was in the ancient southern scheme of things." In these lines Mencken sounded very much like one of his favorite writers, Sherwood Anderson. . . . And when he told the portion of his tale which concerns the demise of the fabled race, Mencken gave his theme epic proportions. "It would be impossible in all history," he wrote, "to match so complete a drying-up of a civilization."[47]

Fitzgerald had to deal with these disputations whenever his characters considered the South and their own identities. The central problem is that character as he understood it was so various that nothing can ever exist as a monad. Everyone thinks differently about the same thing.

Who in fact were the plantocrats? According to a reliable observer who had lived in the Deep South, William Tecumseh Sherman, they included the sons of lawyers, cotton planters, and men about town. They were a leisure class that enjoyed the advantage of traveling abroad and going to colleges in the North. They certainly had a culture of their own—which had little to do with the patronage of literature: "good billiard players and sportsmen, men who never did work and never will. War suits them, and the rascals are brave, fine riders, bold to rashness, and dangerous subjects in every case. They . . . don't bother their brains about the past, present or future. As long as they have good horses, plenty of forage and open country, they are happy. This is a larger class than most men suppose."[48] Sherman suggested that it would be a good idea to kill or imprison all of them in order to make the country safe for the ordinariness of culture, its day-to-day reliance on law and custom. In due course Mencken lost his argument over the virtues of aristocratic readership and patronage. Walter Lippmann pointed out that under any aristocracy writers would never be free of their patrons.[49] And Fitzgerald, who had invested a part of himself in the dispute, had his heroes think more about gain than glory. Except, that is, for Nick Carraway musing on the descent of his clan from Buccleuch; and Gatsby invoking his own ancestors at Oxford; and Philippe, Count of Villefranche, reclaiming his fief and appanage; and Fitzhugh Lee fighting for the Confederacy one last time in Pat Hobby's studio. That is not to mention Littleboy Le Moyne's battle at the New Haven Lawn Club and Ailie Calhoun, whose South never does stop rising again.

Edward Fitzgerald gave his son a romantic vision of the South that stayed with him; Mencken provided him with a historical argument that did not.[50] The latter never convinced Fitzgerald, who disagreed with its sense of *both* Old and New South. That, I think, is why the examples I've cited take the resistant form of comedy. There are particular reasons for this: a natural place to begin is with Freud's reflections on his own work in "An Autobiographical Study," because it appeared from 1923 to 1925.[51] In that piece, Freud connected two things: his sense of the usefulness of marketplace fiction that informs us about authors just as a case history does, and the nature of dreams that were permeated with the "technical methods" of jokes. He concluded that when we see comedy in fiction we should think of "the representation of a thing by its opposite." There was, he added, consistent "displacement" in writing.[52] This does not mean that Fitzgerald read Freud, although it does mean that Freud's diagnosis applies to Fitzgerald. As Fitzgerald matured, Mencken's ideas became the subject of comic dialogue. Two kinds of things happen: A big subject shrinks to its natural size as we overhear its discussion, and we reluctantly come to admire characters whose will may be much larger than their minds. Fitzgerald does use the "technical methods" of jokes—one of which is seeing how long an ideal can stand up in real time and social space.

Fitzgerald's stories address issues raised by Mencken and others convinced that literature should be a criticism of life. Social life is pretentious enough in New York "society" as pictured in "Dice, Brassknuckles & Guitar." There is the sheer, boring emptiness of northern progress in "The Ice Palace," and the moral blankness of great wealth in "The Diamond as Big as the Ritz." But the big issues appear in diminished form. We see the social world through the eyes of individuals who are a bit off center, and it looks comic, not tragic. Characters like Bernice, Jim Powell, even that good citizen John T. Unger are resistant to their small catastrophes. They reverse their situations and change their ideas. And, of course, so does Fitzgerald. He says of a 1921 letter that it is "written in Mencken's manner which I don't mind parodying for St. Paul consumption." He had other thoughts on literary influence, writing in 1924 that *The Beautiful and Damned* "was a false lead . . . a concession to Mencken," and that the next novel would have some "new thinking" in it.[53] Fitzgerald's stories are often about characters who are willful and "rebellious." The phrase comes from "Bernice Bobs Her Hair," referring to the end of belief in a mentor. That coincides with the beginning of belief in the self. The issue of determinism, so loudly debated by Mencken, seems to have been "placed" by two teenagers in "Basil and Cleopatra," one of whom is Fitzgerald incognito: "She felt, too—as even those who disliked him felt—that there was something else in his face—a mark, a hint of destiny, a persistence that was more than will, that was rather a necessity of pressing its own pattern on the world, of having its way."[54]

In 1924, George Santayana (who was read by both Mencken and Edmund Wilson) wrote about the "playful" and "humorous" reconsideration of serious theories. Intuition, he said, is like free play, and it gives us new angles from which to view something that had until then seemed immune to criticism. Ideas are never, he added, "fair portraits" of real things but tend inexorably to become caricatures. It becomes necessary to take serious claims unseriously, allowing us to correct "one impression by another, drawn from the same object." In terms of Fitzgerald's treatment of ideas, the same subject is in fact treated in different ways when Mencken's ideas encounter stubborn and resistant minds. Santayana praised what he called "perpetual tentativeness" in thought—a happier phrase than any I can think of to imply complexity, variousness, and the actual, mercuric operation of the mind.[55] Although there is that remark of Andy's in "The Last of the Belles" about being "unconvinced about anything."[56]

There are many playful reversals in Fitzgerald: Mencken's baying about the end of Old South noblesse becomes the yapping of Harry Bellamy in "The Ice Palace" about New South "degenerates" who are no longer "the true type of Southern aristocrat" (202). Think of the parody of southern conversational style when Daisy Fay Buchanan plays the role of a belle and simply manages to bewilder her cousin Nick. Or of that great moment when Pat

Hobby decides that the life of General Fitzhugh Lee in "A Patriotic Short" needs "a Jewish touch" to make it understandable. Nobody at the meeting, including Pat, knows what he means, although his follow-up might make Mencken or anyone else think twice about how cunning are history's corridors:

> "What do you mean?" demanded Jack Berners quickly.
>
> "Well, I thought—the way things are and all, it would be a sort of good thing to show that there were a number of Jews in it too."
>
> "In what?"
>
> "In the Civil War." Quickly he reviewed his meager history. "They were, weren't they?"
>
> "Naturally," said Berners, with some impatience, "I suppose everybody was except the Quakers."
>
> "Well, my idea was that we could have this Fitzhugh Lee in love with a Jewish girl. He's going to be shot at curfew so she grabs a church bell—"[57]

Pat has in his daily kleptomania snapped up another trifle, the script of *Curfew Shall Not Ring Tonight.*[58] More quick-witted than we think, he has filed away scenes from this silent film. Still, the joke is on Pat because he's a parrot, not an owl. And on Jack Berners who puts up with him. And on the studio that is actually paying for Jack to put up with him. But I don't think that the issue is Hollywood or Jewish heroism in the Confederacy. It's about "the way things are." In America, history is what you want it to be. And right now, in this studio, within this authorial moment, there will be another redefinition of what we think we know. Pat may well be guilty of theft of intellectual property. But the Old South was bound to disappear from our collective mind—along with many dreams about it, including those of H. L. Mencken.[59] Hollywood in its revisionist way may understand the idea of a usable past ("everybody" was involved) better than Mencken ever did. Most important, the people at this meeting know how American culture uses its past. As both Freud and Santayana wrote, the methods of comedy reveal the failings of seriousness.

Fitzgerald's stories about "flappers" or "success" contain subtextual arguments. When "May Day" echoes H. L. Mencken we are intended to know that there is more than one way to look at an idea. We want especially to look at scenes in Fitzgerald that diminish or reverse "serious" subjects. Such scenes in Fitzgerald do just what Freud thought they did: comprise a silent argument. It's important to remember who gets the last word on those grandly disputed subjects of the early 1920s, like "aristocracy," "civilization," and "national letters." To judge by publishing statistics, more people now know about Tom Buchanan's claim to civilization than H. L. Mencken's. What has more powers of conviction, Mencken's account of the Old South or Pat Hobby's take on Fitzhugh Lee and historical certainty? Pat Hobby seems to be more realistic.

Mencken's certainties have not survived, and part of the answer comes from philosophy in his own time. William James wrote that the desire of the self to produce an objective idea was something of a delusion. Every assertion we make and every category we impose are thwarted by processes in our mind "that run the other way." Reasoning is affected by "inconsistencies" and "obstructions" of our own, let alone the slippery objects in our view. So the self can say both "yes and no" at the same time—which James and others believed was intellectually helpful.[60] His conclusion sets the stage for Edmund Wilson's relativity. It bears especially on Fitzgerald's conviction about the value of contradictions. They are embedded in his characters and nothing makes them more psychologically convincing and, I think, humanly accurate.

3
Gerald Murphy and the New Arts

We tend to think of Sara and Gerald Murphy as they have been reconstructed in *Tender Is the Night,* although the story of their connection to F. Scott Fitzgerald is larger and more complex. Gerald Murphy maintained a lifelong dialogue with Fitzgerald, Hemingway, MacLeish, and other writers on the practice and meaning of writing. He influenced Fitzgerald's visual perception of objects and scenes. He had an especially important mentorial role in Fitzgerald's experience of everyday life—as did Sara Murphy, who interrogated his behavior.

There are two enduring conceptions about the Murphys. The first of these has to do with the "art" of living in Antibes in the early 1920s: "The marriage between Gerald—who meticulously planned, intellectualized, and expended great effort in order to make each moment a beautiful event—and Sara—who lived intuitively and impulsively—produced a unique alchemy, by which their daily life became an artistic venture. Together, they created a distinctly modern, elegant style of living that ranged over art, literature, music, theater, fashion, design, gardening, child rearing and entertaining. Virtually no one who shared the pleasure of their company ever forgot the experience."[1] This particular style did have an end in view. Daily life at Villa America included talk about art and ethics that stayed on the minds of Dos Passos, MacLeish, and Fitzgerald for a very long time. However, the subject was private and not public life. Our national consciousness is civic, utilitarian—and always nervous about exceptions. We know that poetry makes nothing happen, but we never tire of asking it to improve us. Edmund Wilson, who praises modernism in *Axel's Castle,* ends by accusing it of being "indifferent" to political action. Yeats, Proust, and Eliot had lost their moral authority—as would anyone shut up "in one's own private world."[2] Wilson should be given his due, but that is a doubtful line of inquiry. As understood by Wittgenstein in *Philosophical Investigations,* the self is the beginning of awareness: "In what sense are my sensations *private*?—Well, only I can know whether I am really in pain; another person can only surmise it. . . . Other people cannot be said to learn of my sensations *only* from my behaviour,—for *I* cannot be said to learn of them. I *have* them."[3] The essential point for Wittgenstein is not that experience remains private—although it may—but that no one else can understand it by making up rules or posing equivalents. Nor can importance simply be assigned.

In the 1920s, the same kind of fluidity that applied to all other values necessarily applied to those governing the experience of art. In fact, John Dewey wrote in 1929 that a theory of experiential art is "not without import" for either criticism or philosophy. The following bears on both Murphy and Fitzgerald:

> The further men go in the concrete the more they are forced to recognize the logical consequences of their controlling assumptions. We owe it to theories of art prevalent to-day in one school of critics that certain implications, long obscured, of the traditional theory of art and nature have been brought to light. Gratitude for this debt should not be stinted because the adherents of the traditional theory . . . [regard] the newer views as capricious heresies, wild aberrations. For these critics, in proclaiming that esthetic qualities in works of fine art are unique, in asserting their separation from not only ev-

> ery thing that is existential in nature but also from all other forms of good, in proclaiming that such arts as music, poetry, painting have characters unshared with any natural things whatsoever—in asserting such things the critics carry to its conclusion the isolation of fine art from the useful.[4]

Dewey was affected by impressionism, which understood the events of everyday life to be a fit subject for painting. He resists the unnamed censorial power of gentility. And although he had conventional tastes in art he takes the modernist position as to its appropriate subjects.[5] Concepts of the art of private life in the 1920s were embedded in public discourse.

In the period 1900–1930, James, Dewey, Bertrand Russell, Santayana, and Alfred North Whitehead all worked on the twinned subjects of art and experience.[6] While respecting conventional ideas they agreed that art should display scenes of ordinary life. All used the term *experience* in conjunction with the term *art.* Santayana especially wrote about personal taste and style. I think he provided Gerald Murphy with ideas and arguments; what he had to say clarifies recollections of Dos Passos, MacLeish, and John Peale Bishop. Here is Santayana on the authority of taste and style:

> This criterion will be natural, personal, autonomous; a circumstance that will give it authority over our own judgment—which is all moral science is concerned about—and will extend its authority over other minds also, in so far as their constitution is similar to ours. . . . It may be some eloquent appreciations read in a book, or some preference expressed by a gifted friend, that may have revealed unsuspected beauties in art or nature; and then, since our own perception was vicarious and obviously inferior in volume to that which our mentor possessed, we shall take his judgments for our criterion.[7]

It would be difficult to overstate either Gerald Murphy's obsessiveness or George Santayana's advice on being obsessive. The former became notorious, as in the picture of Dick Diver on the beach, for laboriously using "the materials at hand" to embody the "simpler virtues" of familial and communal life.[8] That kind of life responded to Santayana's own observations. He did not find it artificial. In fact, Santayana wrote about the "material basis, a soil" for the expression of ideas in a small and personal universe. What was Santayana's extended purpose? "A criterion of taste," he wrote, has "a social career; it hopes to educate and to judge." It has to be logical enough to convince our "interests." It must reappear in the "subsequent judgments" of those who learn it.[9] In rejecting the genteel tradition, Santayana also left behind the entire panoply of patronage and connoisseurship. As he saw it, art was a process and its study was an activity. Gerald Murphy's letters indicate that he closely read *The Last Puritan,* especially its development of personal "education."[10]

The Murphys' life was a form of artistic discipline; technique applied to circumstance. Gerald Murphy thought that the private domain belonged to the new arts.[11] That domain included serious as well as unserious things—the reader of *The Great Gatsby* knows that it is difficult to distinguish between them because they can be the same. In 1924, Cocteau and Diaghilev planned to model a project on the life of the Murphys at Antibes:

> The ballet that resulted, *Le Train bleu,* is about the summer exodus of the beau monde from Paris to the Côte d'Azur and the cult of physical fitness practiced there. (The ballet was named for the express train that took passengers from Paris to the Riviera.) In addition to creating the summer bathing season, the Murphys, especially Gerald, swam miles every day, performed gymnastics and calisthenics, and often danced on

> the beach. Frolicking in the water, yoga, golf, and tennis, all of which are pantomimed in the ballet, were routinely practiced by the Murphys and their guests. A certain amount of "voguing"—striking the right pose and attitude—was part of the Murphys' scene and was also included in the ballet's choreography. . . . Other aspects of the production similarly recalled the Murphys' life in Antibes. Henri Laurens's set brings to mind the newly manufactured portable bathing cabanas the Murphys installed on La Garoupe beach, and Coco Chanel may have based her costume designs on Gerald's innovations in resort wear. The thirty-eight-foot-long curtain featured an enlargement of a gouache painted by Picasso, depicting two gigantic women running on the beach.[12]

Picasso's work in the 1920s coincided with the establishment of Villa America (1923) and the arrival in southern France of Scott and Zelda Fitzgerald (1924). John Richardson's biography of Picasso emphasizes his connection to new, specifically American subjects. They were being addressed by Cole Porter and Murphy, who were doing the ballet *Within the Quota* about "the impact of America—New York, the Wild West, jazz, Hollywood" on an immigrant who becomes a movie star.[13] But a great deal more was involved: scenes photographed at La Garoupe beach were transformed by Picasso to "drawings and paintings . . . idealized images of classical figures on a generalized shore."[14] In the early 1920s, Picasso did portraits, beach scenes like *Three Modern Graces;* still lifes, including *Mandolin and Guitar;* and many drawings of Sara Murphy, including *Reclining Nude with Pearl Necklace.* His works from 1923 to 1925 include *Seated Nude, Women Running on the Beach, The Kiss*—and *The Pipes of Pan,* which depicts Gerald Murphy.[15] Pierre Daix discusses time and place, artist and subjects in a way that helps us understand the ambiguities of *Tender Is the Night:*

Picasso appears, bare chested on the beach of la Garoupe, in a photograph taken by Murphy. He is wearing Sara's pearls. And although he is holding Olga by the hand so that she can assume a ballet attitude, his painting makes this Sara's summer. Not only because of the part the necklace plays in his drawings—notably those of a concert on the beach with panpipes, which will result in one of the most extraordinary classic canvases, *les Flûtes de Pan*—but for his portraits. Two are entirely covered with sand from the beach, on top of which Picasso placed his colors; one of them remained in his collection. It seems impossible not to recognize Sara in most of the female heads done that summer. Fortunately Olga never went to the disorderly jumble of her husband's studio.[16]

Such works record overt and hidden experiences of everyday life. They focus on the perception of place and object. They presume that daily life is a source of art. Richardson states that Picasso understood Gerald Murphy's accomplishments as well as his sexual confusion.[17] Amanda Vaill emphasizes his intellectual authority over Archibald MacLeish and Fitzgerald. He had actually worked with those artists—Satie, Stravinsky, Léger—who were important in Paris. He had been favorably reviewed by Picasso. He knew jazz, photography, and certainly theater and ballet, for which he provided scenery. Murphy often discussed his ideas; MacLeish recalls his perception of colors and images and his running commentary on landscapes.[18] John Dos Passos, at first skeptical, became a convert in Paris:

> Murphy had invited Dos Passos to join him and Fernand Léger for lunch, and afterward they strolled the quais together. Murphy had been studying art with Léger, with whom he now exchanged a lively conversation as they walked, each de-

> lighting in pointing out to the other such things as a tugboat's red funnel, the flukes of an anchor, winches and coils of rope on a deck, the profile of a woman glimpsed through red geraniums in a window box on a passing barge—all viewed for their shapes and colors. Never had Dos Passos' eye taken in so much along the Seine, which had seemed only banal before. . . . Juxtaposed with Léger's "visual fury" was Murphy's rational and discriminating perceptions marked by "mathematical elegance."[19]

Murphy's notebook (ca. 1922–29) often refers to the geometrical shapes of manufactured things. Trevor Winkfield notes that he seems perfectly to understand "the world of objects" but not "the world of nature."[20] That may suggest emotional and intellectual limits. But it may not reveal limits so much as choices—we can see that Fitzgerald treats nature as a backdrop for narration rather than as a subject in itself. Those engineered "common and uncommon things" reproduced by visual art constitute "the world we have made for ourselves" and form the "only common language" of moderns.[21] It is a lonely world in which the landscapes and cityscapes of modernism distance the observer and separate him from the subject.[22] A story like "Jacob's Ladder" will show the lonely crowd—people always en masse—while other works like "May Day" show people connected only by the moment. In *The Great Gatsby* there is no correspondence between numbers of people identified and their organic presence in the story. They are briefly seen (often in a stunning, objectified evocation of appearance or dress or manner) and soon gone.

Fitzgerald, Hemingway, Murphy, and Picasso were all interested in the documentary powers of photography and were often photographed. Picasso relied on photographic prints as well as his own sketches: sending to Gertrude Stein not only a portrait he had done of Olga Khokhlova (whom he would soon marry) but also a note explaining that it was "like a photographic enlargement." Stein answered that it was the best piece of work he had yet done.[23] Fitzgerald wrote enough about lenses to let us know when he intended either movie or still effects. And Gerald Murphy was especially dedicated to photography. Images in Deborah Rothschild's *Making It New* consciously document his daily life. Murphy modeled for Picasso and also for Man Ray, combining two of his major interests, recording the moment and translating it. His own painting shows photographic technique, especially enlargement, without which *Razor* (1924) and *Watch* (1925) would not have been possible. The idiom of his notebooks is that of a photographer who has used a viewfinder for composition.[24] Even when he is himself the subject, the image seems directorial, as in the memorable snapshot of Gerald and Sara dancing on the beach at East Hampton, circa 1915, the year of their engagement.[25] This was done a decade before the first Leica left the factory and—grainy, faded, now in the sepia of its age—remains an accomplishment of the age of slow film and large format.

Murphy's metropolis is that of Fitzgerald and Hemingway. His notebook envisions a large-scale scene around "acetylene welders at work on constructed iron-work, goggles, light-flashes"; *The Sun Also Rises* describes Brett's white face seen as "men were working on the car-tracks by the light of acetylene flares."[26] Cityscape in *The Great Gatsby* features horizontals and verticals in the form of wires and girders; it is permeated by artificial light and has important scenes dominated by the elevated and by geometrical replications of buildings and windows. Here is Winkfield's assessment of *Boatdeck* (1924): "strong, slanting verticals terminated by horizontals . . . the tableau has the cropped compactness of a snapshot. Indeed, Gerald often adopted a photographer's viewpoint in his paintings, and his notebook contains several notations that could serve as ideas for either paintings or photographs. One of the compositions he envisioned, noted on a trip to New York in the fall of 1926, involved a view from the elevated Third Avenue subway looking '*down* into shops, lighted windows . . . *across* at sills and windows, up at roof cornices: 3 perspectives.'"[27] Are these simply details out of which some whole remains to be constructed?

Susan Sontag describes the popularity of this kind of photographic view not only as it is exemplified by the work of Man Ray but also in the enterprises of "painting, theater, and advertising" that shared in the "theatricalization of the real" in the 1920s. She adds that photos inevitably "turn interesting details into autonomous compositions."[28] Man Ray's career was in part based on the isolation of industrial detail—but he and other photographers after the war believed this had actually brought "a sense of wonder back" into the world. For Man Ray, Murphy, and Marcel Duchamp, immersion in rediscovered detail did not by any means signify the defeat of integrated meaning. On the contrary, there was now "a new meaning for each object." The camera lens allowed the exploration of internal space, concentration on natural facts.[29]

Man Ray was closely connected to the Murphys, a frequent consultant in Paris and a frequent visitor at Villa America. He imposed a new kind of form on documentation:

> For the most part, Man Ray portraits took the form of close-ups, like movie stills. He captured James Joyce in profile the moment he turned away from the camera to shield his eyes from the studio lights. Berenice Abbott, then an impoverished sculpture student, appeared only as a face floating in a sea of shadow. . . . Sinclair Lewis, slightly inebriated after the cafés on the boulevard Montparnasse, was seated before a large wooden screw from a wine press—a readymade Brancusi found in an antique shop—Lewis's head and shoulders

> forming the base for the wooden column that towered behind him. The drum of a banjo formed a halo around the face of a young Hemingway newly arrived in Paris.[30]

Man Ray shot the iconic *Gertrude Stein and Picasso's Portrait* in 1922, and, over the next four years, a large number of documentary stills of Sara, Gerald, their children, and the entourage at Villa America. It looks as if Gerald (like Abbott, Brancusi, Picasso, and others) was a student of Man Ray's abstract work. *Boatdeck* is very close to Man Ray's use of "glowing silhouettes of pipes, keys, funnels."[31] *Razor* and other works depend on "tactility" and magnified "space." The list of manufactured things used by Man Ray appears to be a kind of inventory for artists like Murphy—prisms, beads, needle, magnifying glass, and other manufactured objects in changing conditions of light. One thing especially needs to be recalled: things never remain "objects from his own world."[32] His work is certainly about "documentary objectivity," but it also dwells on abstract qualities from which meanings are inferred. His portraits of Nancy Cunard, Jean Cocteau, and Gerald Murphy in the 1920s seem, like the work of Eugène Atget, to show "ostensible ordinariness." But they suggest as much as they depict.[33] Kirk Curnutt's fine analysis of the narrative of *Tender Is the Night* demonstrates how acts differ from intentions—and the degree to which they are theatricalized.[34] In a sense, nothing remains purely documentary, and Man Ray has caught the difference between the outside and the inside of the model.

Murphy encouraged discussion with his friends about meaning as well as artistic technique. We understand from the beginning that concepts like "style of living" and "art of life" are deceptive. Man Ray's work appeared in *Der Querschnitt* and *Variétés,* both of which argued that not only "popular arts" but also "the aesthetic experience" had to be integrated "into everyday life."[35] If anything, that conception is less clear now that popular culture emphasizes *being* rather than *awareness of being*. Today, a particular confusion arises with the rubric of "living well is the best revenge," which became the title of Calvin Tomkins's biography of Sara and Gerald in *The New Yorker* (1962). Gerald proposed it although he knew that it might need to be explained. I agree with Vaill that his source was George Herbert.[36] Herbert used a Spanish proverb but not for its crudely axiomatic truth: he gave it a literary and biographical context. The context matters more than the provenance. The first thing to ask is, why Herbert? The metaphysical poets had become an intellectual presence from the early 1920s on, rediscovered after the publication of John Donne's works by H. J. C. Grierson in 1912. T. S. Eliot's critical essays of the 1920s and '30s established their contemporary importance for modern readers. The basic critical text, *The Poetry of Meditation,* connects Herbert through Eliot to modernism: "I believe there is a direct, a deliberate, relationship between poetry and meditation in the twentieth century. Of Eliot's acquaintance with meditative, or contemplative, writers it is hardly necessary to speak: the commentaries on *Ash Wednesday* and the *Four Quartets* are full of clues."[37] After Eliot, the model of "metaphysical" poetry—intellectual and introspective—replaced "the Romantic and Victorian and Georgian standards."[38] His interpretation emphasized the role of thought above feeling and argued for poetry to be morally informed. By 1962 there had been a great edition of Herbert's work by F. E. Hutchinson and definitive essays about him by L. C. Knights and Eliot. The Knights essay in particular has its own "clues." It discusses Herbert's feelings of "uselessness and self-distrust" and also his "weakness" of will, a term later invoked by Gerald Murphy to explain his own failings.[39]

Knights's essay provides a biographical narrative describing Herbert (like Murphy) as a man who liked "fine clothes and good company" before coming to "regard his own life, the life he was actually leading, as worthless and unprofitable."[40] He was dominated by personal ambition but came to understand that a good life required more than success. In Herbert's own essays, that begins with a wife whose chief aim is "a trayning up of her children." Second, their household should be a living example of personal order imposed on existential chaos. Third, their house, although plain, must be full of hospitality. Finally, a man's goal should be "the improvement of things" in both material and spiritual ways—and as to fare and style, "what hee hath, is little, but very good."[41]

In 1962, T. S. Eliot published the last of his critical works, which was in fact *George Herbert*. Here is Lyndall Gordon on Eliot's "portrait" of Herbert: "a man well-born, proud, and snobbish, meticulous of dress and ambitious of worldly position who, in his thirties, turned aside from the world. . . . With a powerful intellect and by nature not meek, Herbert underwent unsparing self-examination and self-criticism."[42] There was no steady progress toward a resolution in the case of either Murphy or of Herbert, only sequences of rise and fall. These continual failures created problems of conscience.

Fitzgerald, who knew philosophy, stated that Murphy was ethically compelling. He "had come to dictate my relations with other people when these relations were successful: how to do, what to say. How to make people at least momentarily happy. . . . This always confused me and made me want to go out and get drunk, but this man had seen the game, analyzed it and beaten it, and his word was good enough for me."[43] Another witness, Archibald MacLeish, stated that the phrase "living well is the best revenge" was misread by those who came after the fact. It had two components: the practice of art, and living rightly after disillusion.[44] Fitzgerald seems to have understood the range of meanings implicit in "relations with other people." It was a reiterated subject of the Murphy-Fitzgerald correspondence. There is a particular focus, as can be seen in a letter Murphy wrote to Scott in 1925. The letter develops the terms "distinction" and "value" in both art and character: "We four communicate by our presence. . . . Scott will uncover for me values in Sara, just as Sara has known them in Zelda through her affection for Scott."[45] These terms reappear in Gerald's letters and in Scott's fiction.

Linda Patterson Miller has tried from the available evidence to reconstruct issues important to John Peale Bishop, Murphy, MacLeish, and Fitzgerald:

> The conflict that defined much of the era's literature and art, including painting, dance, and music, most often created dissonance rather than artistic resolution. As MacLeish understood well, "the shimmer and sheen of the inventiveness" of the era's art merely succeeded in heightening the "tragic depth of the theme." Ironically, shortly after many of them had begun to gather on the terrace of the Murphys' newly renovated Villa America in 1925, they discussed in the abstract this idea of tragedy. John Peale Bishop's ideas on tragedy had stimulated their thinking, and. . . . Murphy and MacLeish had agreed with this idea. . . . "We are afraid of our own lives."[46]

I take the ending phrase to mean that the conduct of life was a constant subject of artistic discussion. There were different points of view: MacLeish framed his thoughts about the good life around the opposition between art and its imitations. He thought that Hemingway was right about most expatriates, and he praised Bishop and Fitzgerald for "actually working, really producing."[47] That is to say, "inventiveness" really was at the service of "theme." Fitzgerald and Murphy, lapsed but not extinct Catholics, never settled for this Protestant ethic. They were conflicted about the relationship between these quantities. Inventiveness, combining form and insight, might never solve the problem of meaning. And it might have a fairly disastrous connection to relationships.

In an apologetic letter to Sara Murphy for her portrayal in

Tender Is the Night, Fitzgerald wrote that he meant to evoke her, not represent her as a portrait might.[48] "Evocation" characterizes modernist visual art—and also *Tender Is the Night* and *The Great Gatsby.* Art historians have noted that "early modern artists deliberately cultivated a sense of vagueness, generality, or ambiguity, for these qualities enhanced the spiritual, mystical, and universal aspects of their art. Whereas images from earlier periods usually contain telling details in the form of backgrounds, costumes, and other paraphernalia, modern pictures are often remarkably limited in their use of props, concentrating instead on individual figures as distillations or evocations of essential moods or emotions . . . the body remained a central and abiding motif . . . representations of gesture and emotion elicit open-ended, even elusive, readings that often intensify the viewer's desire *to further examine and reflect upon the human condition.*"[49] The passage is clear about the problem of meaning that I have mentioned because it moves decisively from technique to consequence. In this particular case, evocation addresses Fitzgerald's thought about artistic problems and sources. One of the most important things about the Fitzgerald-Murphy friendship was its concentration on things personal and social. Both men spent a great deal of time analyzing not only the form but also the effect and meaning of their work. They were focused on the mutuality of experience.

Certain of Fitzgerald's works invoke the concept of evanescent awareness and are structured, necessarily, upon the passing moment. The phrase itself goes back to Goethe's Faust, who begs for time to stay awhile. Fitzgerald brings romanticism up to date in some specific ways. He visualizes things and people and reasons out their undisclosed value. Even his lesser stories affirm the sudden recognition of human essences. His phrase about Gerald and momentary happiness matters because it alludes to the limits of happiness and *to the nature of experience.* It is not simply that happiness is doomed to be temporary or transient, but that life and fictional versions of it proceed through significant moments of awareness. Gerald himself wrote to Sara that, "I think to myself, 'this is the moment that I should like to give my feelings play, this is when I should be feeling something.'" Feeling is important only when "*communicated*."[50] That is a Fitzgerald theme as well.

Fitzgerald and Murphy were not alone in querying the nature of insight and response: one of the most important contemporary accounts about "realized" time appeared in Alfred North Whitehead's *Science and the Modern World* (1925). Whitehead discussed the connection of time and feeling, concluding that romanticism best expounded the relationship. He thought that Shelley was particularly important in establishing that "nature" is continually "changing, dissolving, transforming." This causes the human observer to realize "the endless, eternal, elusive change of things" and himself to undergo "*a change of inward character.*"[51] We will want to pay particular attention to that last, because Whitehead adds that the great consequence of visualizing is "realisation" of human value. The point of experience as seen by Whitehead is its effect upon both object and self. Here is Whitehead on the concept of "value" as it was first perceived by Wordsworth: "Remembering the poetic rendering of our concrete experience, we see at once that the element of value, of being valuable, of having value, of being an end in itself . . . must not be omitted in any account of an event. . . . 'Value' is the word I use for the intrinsic reality of an event. Value is an element which permeates through and through the poetic view of nature. We have only to transfer to the very texture of realisation in itself that value which we recognize so readily in terms of human life."[52] Ideas about experience and value were important to philosophy from one end of the decade to the other. In 1924, Bertrand Russell (like James, Lippmann, Whitehead, and Dewey) wrote that the solution of ethical problems was an issue for the arts: "to proclaim the ends of life, and make men conscious of their value, is not the business of science; it is the business of the mystic, the artist and the poet."[53] I would not myself file such opinions under "aesthetics." When John Dewey writes about them in 1929 he says that artistic perception of the way things are leads to philosophical understanding of what they mean:

> Meaning may be determined in terms of consequences hastily snatched at and torn loose from their connections; then is prevented the formation of wider and more enduring ideas. Or, we may be aware of meanings, may achieve ideas, that unite wide and enduring scope with richness of distinctions. The latter sort of consciousness is more than a passing and superficial consummation or end: it takes up into itself meanings covering stretches of existence wrought into consistency. It marks the conclusion of long continued endeavor; of patient and indefatigable search and test. The idea is, in short, art and a work of art. . . . It directly liberates subsequent action.[54]

I think this passage needs to be applied to John Peale Bishop's sense of the condition of "our own lives"—and also to the letters of Gerald Murphy and F. Scott Fitzgerald. As Dewey put it, understanding the moment requires not only awareness but also artistic interpretation. His use of "consistency"—we might today use the term *integration*—requires that.

Kirk Curnutt writes that the flapper is theatrical, asserting her claim to attention through performance. Fitzgerald celebrates "performative personality," and warns against "the identity confusion" that is bound to arise.[55] He was both author and object of this kind of advice. Sara Murphy believed that he had no conception of otherness. Knowledge of or consideration for other people's "feelings" and "opinions" were, she wrote to him, "*Completely* left out of your makeup." She adds that everything Fitzgerald said he felt for his wife and daughter was stated in "terms of *yourself*."[56] That is a great weakness—the defining weakness—for any novelist. The Murphys thought this was considerably more than an artistic problem. Perhaps it should be put this way: the artistic problem is enclosed within a larger problem.[57]

Sara and Gerald are intellectually present in *Tender Is the Night*—and also in other works. After 1924, when he began his intense relationship with the Murphys, Fitzgerald wrote about their ideas as well as their personae. "Jacob's Ladder" (1927) evokes the particulars of Gerald Murphy's language and conceptions. The story is about a man in love with an actress half his age who becomes a star and leaves him behind. But the narration involves a good deal more than Hollywood—the text was later quarried by Fitzgerald for several "romantic scenes" in *Tender Is the Night*.[58] One of these is focused on the "moment" that represents for Fitzgerald a new and significant awareness of existence beyond his own: "Hesitating tentatively, he kissed her and again he was chilled by the innocence of her kiss, the eyes that at the moment of contact looked beyond him out into the darkness of the night, the darkness of the world. She did not know yet that splendor was something in the heart; at the moment when she should realize that and melt into the passion of the universe he could take her without question or regret." In a passage that closely follows, Fitzgerald's own ideas about relationship are significantly expanded: "He valued her now more than he had ever thought possible. He watched in her the awakening of a sharply individual temperament. She liked quiet and simple things. She was developing the capacity to discriminate and shut the trivial and the unessential out of her life."[59] These are criteria discussed by both Sara and Gerald Murphy who encouraged awareness, discrimination, and, especially, valuation. In the letter of 1925 that I have mentioned, Gerald wrote to Fitzgerald about the importance of "distinction" and "value" in personal life. Letters to Hemingway and Dos Passos as well as Fitzgerald refer to the substantiation of these things (they are the "subsequent" judgments and actions described by both Dewey and Santayana) through human relationships.

In a letter of 1926, Gerald wrote to Hemingway that "most other people" need to be awakened into a thinking and feeling life; another letter the same year states his admiration for Hadley Richardson Hemingway while criticizing her limits, pointing out that Ernest required an "other" and more reflective self. The same letter is exceptionally useful because Gerald says of himself that "I have thought in values" about the relationship. A letter to MacLeish of 1932 describes the "valueless" nature of life without emotional response; Sara's letter to Fitzgerald in 1934 insists that he become aware of "other people's feelings," while her 1936 letter to him after the publication of "his trilogy in *Esquire*" is a study in moral rage because his self-pity excluded feelings from all other human subjects.[60] These interrogations made their point: in a letter of 1938 in which Fitzgerald reviewed their experience since the 1920s, he stated that he had entered a new phase of expectation: "a development of something that began long ago in my writing—to try to dig up the relevant, the essential, and especially the dramatic and glamorous from whatever life is around." And in an extraordinary coda to this he wrote that his early talent for the depiction of "objective" fact had now been modified—he needed to focus on the self as much as on his "sensory impression of the world."[61]

Fitzgerald had, I think, a long internal debate about such ideas after 1924 extending well past *Tender Is the Night.* It occurs in unexpected places like the Basil and Josephine stories of the late 1920s, and even those about Pat Hobby. Here is a passage from "The Scandal Detectives" (1929). The moment of awareness of this story occurs at "that soft and romantic time" at the end of the day—and also at the end of a stage of life:

> Basil rode over to Imogene Bissel and balanced idly on his wheel before her. Something in his face then must have attracted her, for she looked up at him, looked at him really, and slowly smiled. . . . For a moment Basil was granted an insight into the future; and the spell of her vitality crept over him suddenly. For the first time in his life he realized a girl completely as something opposite and complementary to him, and he was subject to a warm chill of mingled pleasure and pain. It was a definite experience and he was immediately conscious of it. The summer afternoon became lost in her suddenly—the soft air, the shadowy hedges and banks of flowers, the orange sunlight, the laughter and voices, the tinkle of a piano over the way—the odor left all these things and went into Imogene's face as she sat there looking up at him with a smile.[62]

A great deal has happened to the stories since the beginning of the decade. The idea of realization now has an adequate object, and "insight" can, within limits, be applied to "experience." I think, however, that the limits were preponderant.

As Gerald and Sara Murphy reiterated their ideas to Fitzgerald from 1924 on, a steady stream of publications by Freud investigated the effects of teaching and learning values. Freud thought there were only temporary resolutions to "conflicts between the ego and the ideal." That was because such conflicts "reflect the contrast between what is real and what is psychical, between the external world and the internal world." They are not easily resolved in actual experience. On the one hand, Fitzgerald was taught by Gerald and Sara Murphy to divine the value of others and to assert his own. That was necessary to their lives, almost certainly an antidote to their own anxieties. But as if in response to the whole notion of self-improvement "The Ego and the Id" states that our quest for "the higher side of man" begins in fear and ends in failure. Here is Freud on the mentoring process: "It is easy to show that the ego ideal answers to everything that is expected of the higher nature of man. . . . The self-judgement which declares that the ego falls short of its ideal produces the religious sense of humility to which the believer appeals in his longing. As a child grows up, the role of father is carried on by teachers and others in authority; their injunctions and prohibitions remain powerful in the ego ideal and continue, in the form of conscience, to exercise the moral censorship." There are unforeseen but universal consequences: conscience produces guilt along with the temporary resolution of problems in our relationships. Finally, "identifications with other people"—a phrase that asks to be applied to Fitzgerald—often end in hostility.[63] From the beginning, the idea of improvement inculcated by Sara and Gerald Murphy was compromised.

That helps us understand both *Tender Is the Night* and its human sources. The study of narrative by Kirk Curnutt that I have mentioned shows that "self-revision" in *Tender Is the Night* can be illusory: when Dick Diver is attracted to Rosemary, he regresses into "solipsism." His "self-absorption prevents insight," and, in a stunning passage cited from the novel, he plays on "stimulated emotional attention" rather than on authenticity of feeling and style. The narrative is immensely realistic: Kirk Curnutt shows how much "*more* intriguing" that makes Diver to his "entourage."[64] It appears that Gerald Murphy endured the usual mentorial fate. His ideal of emotional authenticity becomes comic theater. His friends—Diver's friends—become in that acute phrase, an "entourage" or audience for whom he performs. In the 1920s and '30s, Murphy hoped to instill in Fitzgerald the awareness of distinction and value in others. Yet Freud had already written that "a social sense" and our respect for admired figures have a short and illusory lifespan.[65]

Fitzgerald's later stories subordinate action to the play of the narrative mind. If the early stories are like shooting Niagara, these are like navigating the Mississippi. In "The Last of the Belles" or "Babylon Revisited" the point is not so much what happens as what has been thought while awaiting it. What an extraordinary moment it is when Andy begins to think about the impossible gradations of sincerity, realizing that it means, finally, the way that Ailie Calhoun "wanted to be regarded." Another story could be written on the foundations of the three or four lines describing Charlie Wales's sense of the independence of his daughter's mind—or on the repetitions of a single word like "gone," which imply not only time but also the self that Fitzgerald in 1924 so badly wanted to leave behind. We're rarely in doubt when reading the earlier stories, but by the 1930s motive and response come in for the attention assumed by act and consequence. At one point Andy says, "I should have made one of those fine moral decisions that people make in books."[66] He begins to understand human inconsistency through himself—while Fitzgerald understands the play of consciousness within the most ordinary of American moments. "The Last of the Belles" keeps looking at time past, but not because of nostalgia. We see things again as they resolve themselves against our will, taking the wrong course inevitably. It is the opposite of Mencken's heroic theory of fiction but has, I think, a better sense of the way things actually happen.

Gerald Murphy was not responsible for Fitzgerald's own discoveries. He had been working on the idea of the essential in human relationships for a very long time. Yet Fitzgerald's work in the period I have mentioned contains themes from the intermittent conversation between Sara and Gerald Murphy and himself. At each stage of his intellectual life, Fitzgerald asked friends and mentors what they thought about ideas and experience; and at each stage he put their insights into (highly critical) narrative form. His dialogue with mentors reappeared in his works. That was not in order to allow himself the last word. Every time the dialogue was framed, it modified itself. The most striking thing about his mind (especially when we think about the directed intelligences of Edmund Wilson and H. L. Mencken) was its power of reconsideration. When he judges Mencken's disciples he states coldly that there are few charms in raw insights. The "data" we begin with needs continual reworking; the writer needs to step out of the "maternal shadow."[67]

Notes

Introduction

1. Wilson, *Literary Essays and Reviews of the 1920s & 30s,* ed. Dabney, 307. In an early letter (1919) Wilson remarked to Fitzgerald that "your artistic conscience . . . was always the weakest part of your talent." In Wilson, *Letters on Literature and Politics, 1912–1972,* ed. Elena Wilson, 44.

2. Wilson, "Prologue, 1952: Christian Gauss as a Teacher of Literature," in *Literary Essays and Reviews of the 1920s & 30s,* ed. Dabney, 17–18.

3. Wilson, "A Weekend at Ellerslie," in ibid., 306, 307, 314. Leon Edel's "Editor's Foreword" to Wilson, *The Twenties,* states that "Edmund used and reused his materials in so many cunning ways," xii.

4. Dabney, *Edmund Wilson: A Life in Literature,* 325.

5. Wilson, "F. Scott Fitzgerald," in *Literary Essays and Reviews of the 1920s & 30s,* ed. Dabney, 30.

6. Fitzgerald, "The Diamond as Big as the Ritz," in *The Short Stories of F. Scott Fitzgerald,* ed. Bruccoli, 215. Millay and Wilson may have been reading although not crediting Santayana. In 1905 he described "an old woman in a blond wig, a dirty hand covered with jewels, ostentation without dignity, rhetoric without cogency, all offend by an inner contradiction . . . the artist has worked in the dark. He has dismissed his work without having quite understood it" (Santayana, "The Criterion of Taste," in *The Essential Santayana,* 323). Matthew J. Bruccoli states of this episode that the Wilson-Millay attack damaged Fitzgerald's reputation for many years. See his *Some Sort of Epic Grandeur,* 161.

7. See Morris Dickstein, "Edmund Wilson: Three Phases," in Dabney, *Edmund Wilson: Centennial Reflections,* 17.

8. Wilson, "Mr. Rolfe," in *Literary Essays and Reviews of the 1930s & 40s,* ed. Dabney, 236.

9. Wilson, *Upstate,* 185.

10. Santayana, "Comparison with Other Criticisms of Knowledge," in *The Essential Santayana,* 125.

11. Fitzgerald, *The Pat Hobby Stories,* 149.

12. Fitzgerald, "In the Darkest Hour," in *The Price Was High: The Last Uncollected Stories of F. Scott Fitzgerald,* ed. Bruccoli, 526.

13. Ibid., 518; *The Pat Hobby Stories,* 27.

14. Fitzgerald, *This Side of Paradise,* ed. West, 260.

15. Wilson, "Mr. Rolfe," in *Literary Essays and Reviews of the 1930s & 40s,* ed. Dabney, 254.

16. Wilson, "Prologue, 1952: Christian Gauss as a Teacher of Literature," 11.

17. Ibid., 15.

18. See Wilson on Mencken, Ring Lardner, Van Wyck Brooks, and the decade, in *Upstate,* 141–42, 182–86. Wilson states, "I felt . . . that the twenties had been a squalid period."

19. See Wilson on Orwell: "He does not belong to the literary world of liberal and radical opinion which has mastered all the right sets of answers and slips easily into all the right attitudes" (Wilson, *From the Uncollected Edmund Wilson,* ed. Groth and Castronovo, 306).

20. Wilson, "Prologue, 1952: Christian Gauss as a Teacher of Literature," 24.

21. Wilson, *Letters on Literature and Politics, 1912–1972,* ed. Elena Wilson, 84.

22. Wittgenstein, *Culture and Value,* 2e, 3e.

23. Dabney, *Edmund Wilson: A Life in Literature,* 129. Emphasis added.

24. Wilson, *The Twenties,* ed. Edel, 183.

25. Berman, *Fitzgerald-Wilson-Hemingway,* 42–74.

26. Wilson, "Prologue, 1952: Christian Gauss as a Teacher of Literature," 14.

27. See Bruccoli, *Some Sort of Epic Grandeur,* 159–60, for Mencken's running account of Fitzgerald's progress as a writer.

28. Mencken, *My Life as Author and Editor,* 259, 309.

29. Wilson's opening passage of "The Early Years" about his own life comes from a 1923 letter to Mencken. Wilson, *Letters on Literature and Politics, 1912–1972,* ed. Elena Wilson, 1.

30. Wilson, in *Literary Essays and Reviews of the 1930s & 40s,* ed. Dabney, 560–61.

31. Ibid., 561–62.

32. Wilson, "Prologue, 1952: Christian Gauss as a Teacher of Literature," 29.

33. See Wilson's elegy to "a past that is now remote" in his Rolfe essay (Wilson, "Mr. Rolfe," in *Literary Essays and Reviews of the 1930s & 40s,* ed.

Dabney, 255): "And I am glad to renew my sense of Alfred Rolfe's contribution to it, as I realize that I myself have been trying to follow and feed it at a time when it has been running low. Its tradition antedates our Christian religion and has in many men's minds survived it; as one may hope it will, also, the political creeds, with their secular evangelism, that are taking the Church's place."

34. Fitzgerald, *Correspondence of F. Scott Fitzgerald,* ed. Bruccoli and Duggan, 70. Dated "Before 7 October 1920."

35. Wilson, "H. L. Mencken," in *Literary Essays and Reviews of the 1920s & 30s,* ed. Dabney, 861–62.

36. In *The Twenties,* Wilson writes that Dos Passos "was, so far as I knew, the first American novelist to make the people of our generation talk as they actually did" (324). See Wilson's passage on "readers of books" who have to undergo "conscious falsification of life" (312–13).

37. Mencken, "Preface to the Fourth Edition," in *The American Language,* vi. Mencken states that he has been working on the subject since 1910.

38. Wilson, "Talking United States," in *Literary Essays and Reviews of the 1920s & 30s,* ed. Dabney, 513–14.

39. Mencken, "The Common Speech," in *The American Language,* 459.

40. Ibid.

41. Davidson, *Subjective, Intersubjective, Objective,* 90.

42. Fitzgerald, "May Day," in *Before Gatsby: The First Twenty-Six Stories,* ed. Bruccoli and Baughman, 311.

43. Wilson, "Talking United States," in *Literary Essays and Reviews of the 1920s & 30s,* ed. Dabney, 518.

44. Fitzgerald, *The Great Gatsby,* ed. Bruccoli, 24–30.

45. Fitzgerald, "Introduction to the Modern Library Reprint of *The Great Gatsby,*" in *F. Scott Fitzgerald on Authorship,* ed. Bruccoli and Baughman, 139.

46. Fitzgerald, "How to Waste Material: A Note on My Generation," in ibid., 106.

47. Mencken, "The Advent of Psychoanalysis," in *H. L. Mencken's Smart Set Criticism,* ed. Nolte, 149, 150, 151. See the sections on "Psychology" (131–56) and "The Critic as Demolition Expert" (157–74). See also "Psychology" (317–28), "Science" (329–42), and "Quackery" (343–67) in *A Mencken Chrestomathy.* Many references to psychology in Mencken's works are not divided into sections nor are they indexed. See Matthew J. Bruccoli's *Some Sort of Epic Grandeur* (236–37) for Mencken's interest in behaviorism.

48. For an account of Mencken's errors see Hobson, *Serpent in Eden: H. L. Mencken and the South,* 16–27. Principal among them was his confusion of the

eighteenth-century South with the pre–Civil War South whose main intellectual activity was the justification of slavery.

49. Mencken, "The Sahara of the Bozart," in *Prejudices: Second Series,* 140.

50. Mencken, "The Anatomy of Ochlocracy," in *H. L. Mencken's Smart Set Criticism,* ed. Nolte, 153.

51. Fitzgerald, *Correspondence of F. Scott Fitzgerald,* ed. Bruccoli and Duggan, 138. To Bernard Vaughan, December 1923.

52. Mencken, *Prejudices: First Series,* 80.

53. Mencken, "The Sahara of the Bozart," in *Prejudices: Second Series,* 137–38; Fitzgerald, "The Offshore Pirate," in *Before Gatsby,* ed. Bruccoli and Baughman, 274, 282.

54. Fitzgerald, *The Beautiful and Damned,* 318.

55. Fitzgerald, *Correspondence of F. Scott Fitzgerald,* ed. Bruccoli and Duggan, 70.

56. Wilson, "H. L. Mencken," in *Literary Essays and Reviews of the 1920s & 30s,* ed. Dabney, 857, 859.

57. In a letter (April 11, 1924) to the editor of *Adventure* (Fitzgerald, *Correspondence of F. Scott Fitzgerald,* ed. Bruccoli and Duggan, 139), Fitzgerald wrote that although *The Beautiful and Damned* was "a better book" than *This Side of Paradise,* "it was a false lead . . . a concession to Mencken."

58. Fitzgerald, "How to Live on Practically Nothing a Year," in *My Lost City: Personal Essays, 1920–1940,* ed. West, 41.

59. Fitzgerald, *A Life in Letters,* ed. Bruccoli, 84.

60. Mellow, *Invented Lives,* 203: "When MacLeish first met the couple, he thought them strikingly 'well-laundered' and was eager to know them. If the Murphys had been slightly older, they might well have passed for Fitzgerald's ideal parents. They were wealthy, well-bred, and handsome. Their cultural interests ranged far more widely than his own; they appreciated the vanguard compositions of Les Six and the musical comedies of their friend Cole Porter, and introduced Negro spirituals to their French friends. They had distinctive good taste when it came to wine and food; everything they did had style—whether it was serving cocktails, furnishing a house, or giving a party."

61. Santayana, "The Criterion of Taste," in *The Essential Santayana,* 324.

62. There are extensive references to the Murphys in Blazek and Rattray, *Twenty-First-Century Readings of* Tender Is the Night, especially Michael K. Glenday, "American Riviera: Style and Expatriation in *Tender Is the Night,*" 143–59.

63. Rothschild, *Making It New: The Art and Style of Sara and Gerald Murphy.*

64. Cited by Rothschild, "Masters of the Art of Living," in *Making It New,* 43.

65. Elizabeth Hutton Turner, "Transatlantic," in Foresta, *Perpetual Motif: The Art of Man Ray,* 154.

66. Ibid., 152, 160; Rothschild, *Making It New,* 34, 58, 110, 113. See "Exhibition Checklist for Fine Art," in *Making It New,* 213–15.

67. Sandra S. Phillips, "Themes and Variations: Man Ray's Photography in the Twenties and Thirties," in Foresta, *Perpetual Motif: The Art of Man Ray,* 195.

68. Santayana, "The Moral Background," in *The Genteel Tradition: Nine Essays by George Santayana,* ed. Wilson, 91–92.

69. Ibid., 25, cited by Douglas A. Wilson, "Introductory," in *The Genteel Tradition.*

70. For gentility in art see Wood, *Empire of Liberty: A History of the Early Republic, 1789–1815,* 543–75. See especially 560–61 on "morally instructive art." Wood notes that the more efforts were made to bring art to the public, the more it became an instrument of civic virtue.

71. Richardson, *A Life of Picasso: The Triumphant Years, 1917–1932,* 205. Citation from Calvin Tomkins, *Living Well Is the Best Revenge.* See my discussion of Fitzgerald and poster art in *The Great Gatsby and Modern Times,* 94–97.

72. Richardson, *A Life of Picasso,* 228.

73. Miller, *Letters from the Lost Generation,* xxviii.

74. Ibid.

75. Eliot, "Andrew Marvell," in *Selected Essays,* 256, 257.

76. See William Jay Smith, "Gerald Murphy: Cubist Painter, Concrete Poet," in Rothschild, *Making It New,* 185: "His greatest paintings, *Watch* and *Wasp and Pear* . . . depict with great objectivity and precision the triumph of time and death. The depiction is epitomized in MacLeish's famous poem 'You, Andrew Marvell,' which Gerald Murphy must certainly have known."

77. Rothschild, "Masters of the Art of Living," in *Making It New,* 60.

78. Phillips, "Themes and Variations," in Foresta, *Perpetual Motif: The Art of Man Ray,* 199.

79. See the excellent account of "troubled" psychology in Miller, *Letters from the Lost Generation,* xxix–xxxi.

80. Smith, "Gerald Murphy: Cubist Painter, Concrete Poet," in Rothschild, *Making It New,* 186.

81. Miller, *Letters from the Lost Generation,* 140.

82. Cited by Bruccoli, *Some Sort of Epic Grandeur,* 200.

83. Scholarly studies of *Tender Is the Night* have been concerned with Fitzgerald's use of psychiatry. Among the best of them are William Blazek, "'Some Fault in the Plan': Fitzgerald's Critique of Psychiatry in *Tender Is the Night,*" and Philip McGowan, "Reading Fitzgerald Reading Keats," in Blazek and Rattray, *Twenty-First-Century Readings of* Tender Is the Night, 67–84, 204–20. I have not dealt with Freud's clinical work except in passing, but with his thoughts on cultural ideas, institutions, and relationships.

84. See Scottie Fitzgerald Smith, in Bruccoli, Smith, and Kerr, *The Romantic Egoists,* x: "We use the word "egoist," of course, in a literary sense and not as a term of disparagement. More than most authors, my father drew on his personal experience, both trivial and tragic, for his fiction and his nonfiction."

85. Wilson, *Edmund Wilson: The Man in Letters,* ed. Castronovo and Groth, 70.

86. Wittgenstein, *Culture and Value,* 1e.

Chapter 1

1. Dabney, *Edmund Wilson: A Life in Literature,* 49.

2. For Wilson's assessment of Fitzgerald (and an assessment of Wilson) see Bruce L. Grenberg, "Fitzgerald's 'Crack-up' Essays Revisited: Fictions of the Self, Mirrors for a Nation," in Bryer, Margolies, and Prigozy, *F. Scott Fitzgerald: New Perspectives,* 204.

3. Wilson, *Letters on Literature and Politics, 1912–1972,* ed. Elena Wilson, 73. See Dabney, *Edmund Wilson: A Life in Literature,* 122–23 for Wilson's view of Fitzgerald's intellectual discipline, which sometimes caused him to lose "control over his material."

4. Fitzgerald, "My Lost City," in *My Lost City,* ed. West, 106.

5. Wilson, *Letters on Literature and Politics, 1912–1972,* ed. Elena Wilson, 127.

6. Trilling, "Edmund Wilson: A Backward Glance," in *A Gathering of Fugitives,* 50.

7. Wilson, *The American Earthquake,* 11: *TAE* is "a selection from my nonliterary articles written during the twenties and thirties," which "runs more or less parallel to the literary material collected in my earlier volume, *The Shores of Light.*"

8. Ibid., 59.

9. See Dabney, *Edmund Wilson: A Life In Literature,* 124: "Like Cum-

mings, Dos Passos, Robert Benchley, and Frank Crowninshield," Wilson visited "the Minskys' burlesque." Many writers of the 1920s were familiar with revues and got their information about Broadway first hand. However, Wilson published his experience and was rightly considered to be a source of ideas about New York. In the early 1930s, Dos Passos wrote an enthusiastic review of *The American Jitters,* stating that it had "a great deal of valuable information." Cited by Carr, *Dos Passos: A Life,* 326. Such information can be seen in Wilson, "Gilbert Seldes and the Popular Arts," in *Literary Essays and Reviews of the 1920s & 30s,* ed. Dabney, 137–38.

10. Lawrence is cited by Carr in *Dos Passos: A Life,* 215.

11. Fitzgerald, *The Great Gatsby,* ed. Bruccoli, 81, 106. See Lathbury, *Literary Masterpieces,* vol. 1, *The Great Gatsby,* 190: "Elevated: the part of the New York subway system that ran on trestles above the streets."

12. Wilson, "Gilbert Seldes and the Popular Arts," in *Literary Essays and Reviews of the 1920s & 30s,* ed. Dabney, 139.

13. Ibid., 36.

14. Ibid., 33–34; Wilson, *The American Earthquake,* 51.

15. Wilson, *Letters on Literature and Politics, 1912–1972,* ed. Elena Wilson, 117.

16. Wilson, *Literary Essays and Reviews of the 1920s & 30s,* ed. Dabney, 205.

17. Wilson, *The American Earthquake,* 87.

18. Edel, in Wilson, *The Twenties,* ed. Edel, 6.

19. Prigozy, "'Poor Butterfly': F. Scott Fitzgerald and Popular Music," 41, 55. See Prigozy, "From Griffith's Girls to *Daddy's Girl:* The Masks of Innocence in *Tender Is the Night,*" 189–221. See also Prigozy, "Fitzgerald's Flappers and Flapper Films of the Jazz Age: Behind the Morality," 129–61.

20. Prigozy, "Fitzgerald's Flappers and Flapper Films of the Jazz Age," 129.

21. Wilson, "The Follies as an Institution," in *The American Earthquake,* 51. See Graham, "Fitzgerald's 'Riotous Mystery': *This Side of Paradise* as Musical Theater," 31. See also Lauraleigh O'Meara, "Symbols of New York: *This Side of Paradise,*" in *Lost City: Fitzgerald's New York,* 13, for the use of Broadway as an indicator of sexual feelings—and intentions.

22. Snyder, *The Voice of the City,* 148–52.

23. Bishop and Wilson, *The Undertaker's Garland,* 18–19.

24. Wilson, *The Twenties,* ed. Edel, 6.

25. Wilson, *Letters on Literature and Politics, 1912–1972,* ed. Elena Wilson, 64.

26. Bruccoli, *Some Sort of Epic Grandeur,* 344. Fitzgerald used the term originally in "Pasting It Together," one of the essays in *The Crack-Up:* "For twenty years a certain man had been my intellectual conscience. That was

Edmund Wilson" (79). See the analysis of Fitzgerald's concept of conscience by Scott Donaldson, *Fitzgerald and Hemingway: Works and Days,* 167–68.

27. In "An Autobiographical Study," Freud wrote that "the super-ego is the heir of the Oedipus complex and represents the ethical standards of mankind" (*The Freud Reader,* ed. Gay, 37).

28. Freud, *Civilization and Its Discontents,* ed. Strachey, 100. The passage applies to Fitzgerald's letters mentioning Wilson's demands and the market realities of his own career: "The super-ego is an agency which has been inferred by us, and conscience is a function, which we ascribe, among other functions, to that agency. This function consists in keeping a watch over the actions and intentions of the ego and judging them, in exercising a censorship. The sense of guilt, the harshness of the super-ego, is thus the same thing as the severity of the conscience. It is the perception which the ego has of being watched over in this way, the assessment of tension between its own strivings and the demands of the super-ego."

29. Wilson, "The Triple Thinkers: Morose Ben Jonson," in *Literary Essays and Reviews of the 1930s & 40s,* ed. Dabney, 213–32. Cited passage, 220. See the brief discussion of Freud by David Bromwich, "Wilson's Modernism," in Dabney, *Edmund Wilson: Centennial Reflections,* 47–48. Jonson scholars have been hospitable to Wilson's view but not bowled over by it. They point out that many writers, including Shakespeare, depicted resentful, masochistic, or even anal characters because it was conventional to do so. Comedy was based on the theory of "humours," hence characters like Shylock and the great eccentrics of Restoration comedy. Wilson scholars are familiar with the comparison I have drawn between him and Jonson because it has become a biographical motif.

30. Wilson, "The Wound and the Bow: The Kipling That Nobody Read," in *Literary Essays and Reviews of the 1930s & 40s,* ed. Dabney, 354.

31. See Turnbull, *Scott Fitzgerald,* 59: "Wilson was a born intellectual whose love of books and culture had led him to explore the surrounding life. Fitzgerald wasn't really an intellectual at all; his talents were of a different order. He had begun with a quick, instinctive love of life and, working in the opposite direction from Wilson, had found his way back to books. From this fundamental antithesis sprang other differences. . . . Compared to Fitzgerald . . . Wilson seemed self-conscious, pedantic, a bit of a priss."

32. See Edward J. Gleason, "Going toward the Flame: Reading Allusions in the *Esquire* Stories," in Bryer, Margolies, and Prigozy, *F. Scott Fitzgerald: New Perspectives,* 216, for a "pattern of references" revealing "a story-beneath-the stories."

33. Freud, "Fragment of an Analysis of a Case of Hysteria ('Dora')," in *The Freud Reader,* ed. Gay, 200.

34. George Santayana, "William James," in *Character and Opinion in the United States,* 44–45.

35. Turnbull, *Scott Fitzgerald,* 103.

36. Fitzgerald, *Correspondence of F. Scott Fitzgerald,* ed. Bruccoli and Duggan, 79. Assigned date is "9 February 1921." Specified date is "Feb 9th 1920."

37. See Bruccoli, *Some Sort of Epic Grandeur,* 41–51, for an account of Fitzgerald's introduction to writers and their ideas at Princeton.

38. Wittgenstein, *The Wittgenstein Reader,* ed. Kenny, 97, 101.

39. Freud, "Contribution to a Questionnaire on Reading," in *The Freud Reader,* ed. Gay, 539–40. Freud chose Kipling's *Jungle Book* over *Faust* or *Hamlet.*

40. Fitzgerald, *Correspondence of F. Scott Fitzgerald,* ed. Bruccoli and Duggan, 25 (January 1918).

41. Fitzgerald, *A Life in Letters,* ed. Bruccoli, 460–61.

42. Graham, *Beloved Infidel,* 240. See LaVerne Kennevan Maginnis, "An Index to *College of One: The Education of a Woman,*" *The F. Scott Fitzgerald Review* 1 (2002): 107–21.

43. Fitzgerald, *Correspondence of F. Scott Fitzgerald,* ed. Bruccoli and Duggan, 80 (9 February 1921); 81 (February 1921).

44. Fitzgerald, *This Side of Paradise,* ed. West, 126, 245.

45. Lippmann, *Public Opinion,* 16–18. Lippmann's passage on empiricism takes up the methods of Freudian analysis applied to "the maladjustment of distinct individuals to other individuals and to concrete circumstances."

46. Fitzgerald, "The Freshest Boy," in *The Basil and Josephine Stories,* ed. Bryer and Kuehl, 67. Future references to this text in parenthesis.

47. Lippmann, *Public Opinion,* 167–68.

48. Freud, "Civilization and Its Discontents," in *The Freud Reader,* ed. Gay, 756–57.

49. Fitzgerald, "Bernice Bobs Her Hair," in *The Short Stories of F. Scott Fitzgerald,* ed. Bruccoli, 33.

50. See the 1923 interview by B. F. Wilson, "F. Scott Fitzgerald Says: 'All Women Over Thirty-five Should Be Murdered,'" in *Conversations with F. Scott Fitzgerald,* ed. Bruccoli and Baughman, 57: "Then Freud came into existence. He has had the widest influence on the younger generation. You cannot begin to conceive how far his theories have spread in America. . . . Why, Freud at third-hand ran over this country like wildfire. He gave the wealthy young girls something new in the way of sensationalism."

51. Wittgenstein, *The Wittgenstein Reader,* ed. Kenny, 107.

52. Fitzgerald, "Bernice Bobs Her Hair," in *The Short Stories of F. Scott Fitzgerald,* ed. Bruccoli, 36.

53. Freud, "On Narcissism: An Introduction," in *The Freud Reader,* ed. Gay, 555.

54. Wilson, "The Delegate from Great Neck," in *Literary Essays and Reviews of the 1920s & 30s,* ed. Dabney, 130.

55. Freud, "The Ego and the Id," in *The Freud Reader,* ed. Gay, 657.

56. See Mencken, *The American Language,* 265.

57. Lewis, *Arrowsmith; Elmer Gantry; Dodsworth,* 652. Elmer works with "many a hesitating boy" who needs masculine guidance in order to "learn the benefits of religion" (678). The novel was published in 1927, the year before this Basil story.

58. Fitzgerald, *Correspondence of F. Scott Fitzgerald,* ed. Bruccoli and Duggan, 436 (June 26 [1936]).

59. In Wilson, *The Twenties,* ed. Edel, 5.

60. Gordon, *T. S. Eliot: An Imperfect Life,* 147–48. Eliot citation from the ending of his essay on "John Ford."

61. Fitzgerald, *The Short Stories of F. Scott Fitzgerald,* ed. Bruccoli, 22.

Chapter 2

1. See H. R. Stoneback, *Reading Hemingway's* The Sun Also Rises, 87–88; Hobson, *Mencken: A Life,* 275–76.

2. Wilson, "Mencken's Democratic Man," in *Literary Essays and Reviews of the 1920s & 30s,* ed. Dabney, 244.

3. Fitzgerald, *Correspondence of F. Scott Fitzgerald,* ed. Bruccoli and Duggan, 138. To Bernard Vaughan (December 1923). Emphasis added.

4. Teachout, *The Skeptic: A Life of H. L. Mencken,* 200–202. Cited passage, 201.

5. Fitzgerald, "How I Would Sell My Book If I Were a Bookseller" (1923), in *F. Scott Fitzgerald on Authorship,* ed. Bruccoli and Baughman, 78.

6. See Sharon Hamilton, "Mencken and Nathan's *Smart Set* and the Story behind Fitzgerald's Early Success," *The F. Scott Fitzgerald Review* 4 (2005): 20–48. "Mencken and Nathan brought Fitzgerald's stories to the right readers, and they seem to have done so throughout the entire two-year period of Fitzgerald's early success" (40).

7. Fitzgerald, *F. Scott Fitzgerald on Authorship,* ed. Bruccoli and Baughman, 174. See Mencken's comparison of the *Post* in 1920 with "such magazines as the *Cosmopolitan, Hearst's, McClure's* and the *Metropolitan.*" Mencken

thought that the *Post* was then the place to find "very solid talents." Mencken, "In the Literary Abattoir," in *Prejudices: Second Series,* 34–35.

8. Thomas Alexander Boyd, "Literary Libels: Francis Scott Key Fitzgerald," in Fitzgerald, *Conversations with F. Scott Fitzgerald,* ed. Bruccoli and Baughman, 14. Fitzgerald states in this interview: "I don't think *Main Street* would have been written if Mencken hadn't been born."

9. See Berman, "'The Diamond' and the Declining West," in *Fitzgerald, Hemingway, and the Twenties,* 40–47.

10. Mencken, "Taking Stock," in *H. L. Mencken's Smart Set Criticism,* ed. Nolte, 318–19.

11. Mencken, *Prejudices: Second Series,* 22–24.

12. See Mencken, *My Life as Author and Editor,* 256–66; Fitzgerald, "Introduction to the Modern Library Reprint of *The Great Gatsby,*" in *F. Scott Fitzgerald on Authorship,* ed. Bruccoli and Baughman, 139.

13. Fitzgerald, *Correspondence of F. Scott Fitzgerald,* ed. Bruccoli and Duggan ("Before 7 October 1920"), 70.

14. Williams, *H. L. Mencken Revisited,* 52–53.

15. Ibid., 35. Williams cites *The Smart Set,* January 1911.

16. Mencken, *Prejudices: Second Series,* 18, 65, 72.

17. Cerasulo, *Authors Out Here: Fitzgerald, West, Parker, and Schulberg in Hollywood,* 145–62.

18. Bruccoli, *Classes on F. Scott Fitzgerald,* 60–61.

19. Fitzgerald, *Correspondence of F. Scott Fitzgerald,* ed. Bruccoli and Duggan, 70.

20. I am indebted to Vincent Fitzpatrick, curator of the Mencken Collection at the Enoch Pratt Free Library of Baltimore, for pointing out the enormous extent of Mencken's recycling. He has made some of the earlier sources available to me and has pointed out Mencken's remarks on "reprints" in Adler, *H. L. M.: The Mencken Bibliography,* 10. Some of Mencken's thoughts on artists are in the *Evening Mail,* April 19, 1918, and in the *Smart Set,* February 1918. Hobson points out in *Serpent in Eden* (24) that the famous essay on "The Sahara of the Bozart" appeared in the New York *Evening Mail,* November 13, 1917.

21. Mencken, *Prejudices: Second Series,* 83.

22. Ibid., 88. Mencken's references to "The Divine Afflatus" antedate *Prejudices: Second Series.* See the New York *Evening Mail,* November 16, 1917; the *Smart Set,* February 1919, and June 1920.

23. Mencken, "Diagnosis of Our Cultural Malaise," in *H. L. Mencken's Smart Set Criticism,* ed. Nolte (February 1919), 4.

24. Mencken did not invent the dilemma of our decadent "civilization." His was a skirmish in a larger war. See Richard Overy's history of British angst, *The Morbid Age,* 7: "this is in no sense an insular history, but a history of ideas and attitudes generated in Britain but then rapidly and widely disseminated in America and Europe."

25. Fitzgerald, *A Life in Letters,* ed. Bruccoli, 41.

26. Fitzgerald, *Before Gatsby: The First Twenty-Six Stories,* ed. Bruccoli, 316. Future page references in parentheses in my text.

27. For Fitzgerald's use of the artist's—and his own—"professional failures," see Petry, *Fitzgerald's Craft of Short Fiction,* 67.

28. Mencken, *Prejudices: Second Series,* 54. "The Lonesome Artist" is one of the ten main sections of "The National Letters" sequence.

29. Mencken, *H. L. Mencken's Smart Set Criticism,* ed. Nolte, 5. This passage was reprinted in *Prejudices: Second Series,* 97. For insight into Mencken's critical attitude, see Sklar, *F. Scott Fitzgerald,* 86.

30. See Williams, *H. L. Mencken Revisited,* 47, on the "tendency of American intellectuals, to use the war to focus attention on the social and cultural tensions within their own society."

31. Mencken, *Prejudices: Second Series,* 73.

32. Mencken, *Notes on Democracy,* 37. See Marion Elizabeth Rodgers's, "Introduction," 10–11: This 1926 book—"the culmination of Mencken's thinking about democracy and the American character"—took its origin from "a series of articles which ran in the *Smart Set* from June through October 1913."

33. Wilson, "Mencken's Democratic Man," in *Literary Essays and Reviews of the 1920s & 30s,* ed. Dabney, 243. See Santayana, *The Essential Santayana,* 104–9 on the resemblance between history and fiction.

34. Wilson, "The Delegate from Great Neck," *Literary Essays and Reviews of the 1920s & 1930s,* ed. Dabney, 130–31.

35. James, "The Self," in *The Philosophy of William James,* 127–28. Emphasis in original.

36. Wilson, "Mencken's Democratic Man," in *Literary Essays and Reviews of the 1920s & 30s,* ed. Dabney, 245. Emphasis added.

37. Mencken, "A Definition," *H. L. Mencken's Smart Set Criticism,* ed. Nolte, 34–35.

38. Mencken, "A Novel of the First Rank," in *A Second Mencken Chrestomathy,* ed. Teachout, 319. See Stenerson, *H. L. Mencken: Iconoclast from Baltimore,* 130: "In the drama and the novel, he called for a realistic or naturalist treatment of American themes, but he also welcomed romance, fantasy, or burlesque." Stenerson states that at the heart of his work was a "preoccupation

with American life." See Trilling, "Edmund Wilson: A Backward Glance," in *A Gathering of Fugitives,* 53: "the belief in a national moral destiny, which marked liberal social and political opinion after the first war, complemented and gave weight to the sense of a developing American culture."

39. Trilling, "Manners, Morals, and the Novel," in *The Moral Obligation to Be Intelligent,* 112.

40. John Dewey, "Experience, Nature, and Art," in *The Philosophy of John Dewey,* ed. McDermott, 323. See 324: "But it still remains that the origin of the art-process lay in emotional responses spontaneously called out by a situation occurring without any reference to art, and without 'esthetic' quality save in the sense in which all immediate enjoyment and suffering is esthetic."

41. Bruccoli, *Some Sort of Epic Grandeur,* 160.

42. Freud, "Creative Writers and Day-Dreaming," in *The Freud Reader,* ed. Gay, 440.

43. Mencken, *Prejudices: Second Series,* 40.

44. Freud, "Creative Writers and Day-Dreaming," in *The Freud Reader,* ed. Gay, 437–40.

45. Fitzgerald, *A Life in Letters,* ed. Bruccoli, 47.

46. Ibid., 111.

47. Hobson, *Serpent in Eden,* 15–16.

48. Cited by Groom in *Vicksburg, 1863,* 34.

49. Lippmann, *Public Persons,* 78–79.

50. See Scott Donaldson, "Fitzgerald's Romance with the South," in *Fitzgerald and Hemingway: Works and Days,* 51–60. See also Fitzgerald's assessment of "before-the-war culture" in the South in an interview of 1922: John O'Donnell, "Fitzgerald Condemns St. Paul Flappers," in Fitzgerald, *Conversations with F. Scott Fitzgerald,* ed. Bruccoli and Baughman, 31.

51. In a 1923 interview Fitzgerald stated that flappers did not understand their own "exuberant vitality" as the 1920s began: "Then Freud came into existence. He has had the widest influence on the younger generation." B. F. Wilson, "F. Scott Fitzgerald Says: 'All Women over Thirty-five Should Be Murdered,'" in Fitzgerald, *Conversations with F. Scott Fitzgerald,* ed. Bruccoli and Baughman, 57.

52. Freud, "An Autobiographical Study," in *The Freud Reader,* ed. Gay, 40.

53. Fitzgerald, *Correspondence of F. Scott Fitzgerald,* ed. Bruccoli and Duggan. To Thomas Boyd (Sept 19th 1921), 85; To Moran Tudury ("Postmarked 11 April 1924"), 139.

54. Fitzgerald, *The Basil and Josephine Stories,* ed. Bryer and Kuehl, 172.

55. Santayana, "The Watershed of Criticism," in *The Essential Santayana,*

84–85. See Frederick Wegener, "The 'Two Civil Wars' of F. Scott Fitzgerald," in Bryer, Prigozy, and Stern, *F. Scott Fitzgerald in the Twenty-First Century,* 245. Wegener discusses the "playful" treatments of the Civil War in the fiction.

56. Fitzgerald, "The Last of the Belles," in *The Short Stories of F. Scott Fitzgerald,* ed. Bruccoli, 453.

57. Fitzgerald, "A Patriotic Short," in *The Pat Hobby Stories,* 116.

58. The 1867 narrative poem *Curfew Must Not Ring Tonight* by Rose Hartwick Thorpe is about a young woman caught up in the wars of Cromwell's time. Her lover has been condemned to die at curfew, so she resolutely climbs the church tower and prevents the bell from ringing. The poem was made into a silent film (*Curfew Shall Not Ring Tonight*) in 1926. The verse original was a favorite of Queen Victoria, and the film version is still rocketing around Pat Hobby's mind. But Pat never does get around the improbabilities of Jewish girls in churches or lining up a firing squad in the dark. See Duane V. Maxey, "The Story of *Curfew Must Not Ring Tonight,*" at http://en.wikipedia.org/wiki/Curfew_Must_Not_Ring_Tonight.

59. It is worth following Edmund Wilson's changing opinions of Mencken. See Wilson, "H. L. Mencken" (1921); "The All-Star Literary Vaudeville" (1926); and "Mencken's Democratic Man" (1926), in *Literary Essays and Reviews of the 1920s & 1930s,* ed. Dabney, 857–64, 191–205, 242–45. For an overview, see Dabney, *Edmund Wilson: A Life in Literature,* 74–75.

60. Gerald E. Myers, "Self," in *William James: His Life and Thought,* 346. Citation from *Principles of Psychology.*

Chapter 3

1. Rothschild, "Masters of the Art of Living," in *Making It New,* 11.

2. Wilson, "Axel's Castle," in *Literary Essays and Reviews of the 1920s & 30s,* ed. Dabney, 837–38. See Rothschild, "Masters of the Art of Living," in *Making It New* (75), for information about Gerald and Sara Murphy's financial support of many artists on the way up—or down. This constituted a vocation in itself.

3. Wittgenstein, "Private Language and Private Experience," in *The Wittgenstein Reader,* ed. Kenney, 142.

4. Dewey, "The Metaphysics of Experience," in *The Philosophy of John Dewey,* ed. McDermott, 322–23.

5. See the verdict of J. K. Huysmans on Manet's *Chez le père Lathuille:* "this canvas catches the eye because [it shows] the modernism that I have spoken about! People eating lunch in real light, in the open air . . . life shown

as it is, without exaggeration." Cited by Chatelain and Hoving in *Impressionism: A Centenary Exhibition,* 129. See also Ryan, *John Dewey and the High Tide of American Liberalism,* 253–54: "Dewey shared the urge to bring into the light of modern critical interest many things that had not been thought of as anything more than anthropologically interesting curios. Benin bronzes; Oceanic carvings; 'primitive' art generally."

6. I have in mind especially Santayana's *Reason in Art* (volume 4 of *The Life of Reason* [1905]); Whitehead's *Science and the Modern World* (1953 [1925]); and Dewey's *Experience and Nature* (1929). Edmund Wilson referred often to Whitehead. Dabney's *Edmund Wilson: A Life in Literature* cites Wilson's belief that "Santayana embodies the priesthood of literature" (325).

7. Santayana, "The Criterion of Taste," in *The Essential Santayana,* 321–22.

8. Fitzgerald, *Tender Is the Night,* 21.

9. Santayana, "The Criterion of Taste," in *The Essential Santayana,* 322, 324. This 1905 essay discusses one of the subjects of Fitzgerald's text—"mastery of existence achieved at one moment"—and Nature's indifference to it.

10. Miller, *Letters from the Lost Generation,* 168, 170, 175, 176.

11. See the discussion of "the moral status of art" in *The Princess Casamassima.* Trilling, *The Moral Obligation to Be Intelligent,* 166.

12. Rothschild, "Masters of the Art of Living," in *Making It New,* 49.

13. Richardson, *A Life of Picasso: The Triumphant Years, 1917–1932,* 238.

14. Rothschild, "Masters of the Art of Living," in *Making It New,* 51, 52.

15. See Picasso, *Pablo Picasso, 1881–1973,* ed. Walther, 292, 293, 299, 300.

16. Daix, *Picasso: Life and Art,* 182–83.

17. Richardson, *A Life of Picasso: The Triumphant Years, 1917–1932,* 239.

18. Vaill, *Everybody Was So Young,* 150–52.

19. Carr, *Dos Passos: A Life,* 195.

20. Winkfield, "The Notebook as Sketchbook," in *Making It New,* ed. Rothschild, 138–39.

21. Peter Reed, "Common and Uncommon Things," in Elderfield, Reed, Chan, and González, eds., *ModernStarts: People, Places, Things,* 297. Citation from Michael Craig-Martin, *A Retrospective, 1968–1989,* 112.

22. Chan and González, "Modern Places," in Elderfield, Reed, Chan, and González, eds., *ModernStarts: People, Places, Things,* 177. Citation from Bradbury and McFarlane, *Modernism.*

23. Richardson, *A Life of Picasso: The Triumphant Years, 1917–1932,* 76.

24. Winkfield, "The Notebook as Sketchbook," in *Making It New,* ed. Rothschild, 137.

25. Rothschild, "Making It New," in *Making It New,* 10.

26. Hemingway, *The Sun Also Rises,* 30. See the discussion of Murphy and cited passage by Miller, "Gerald Murphy in Letters, Literature, and Life," in *Making It New,* ed. Rothschild, 159–61.

27. Winkfield, "The Notebook as Sketchbook," in *Making It New,* ed. Rothschild, 135–37.

28. Sontag, *On Photography,* 52, 147.

29. Herbert Molderings, "Photography as Consolation," in Man Ray, *Man Ray: Photographs,* 14–15. Citation from Pierre Bost, *Photographies modernes.*

30. Elizabeth Hutton Turner, "Transatlantic," in Foresta, *Perpetual Motif: The Art of Man Ray,* 155–56.

31. Ibid., 145.

32. Sandra S. Phillips, "Themes and Variations: Man Ray's Photography in the Twenties and Thirties," in Foresta, *Perpetual Motif: The Art of Man Ray,* 184. Man Ray had in 1922 embarked on the study of refracted light from "crystals," "prisms," and fragmented surfaces (185). His research on variations of light was extravagantly praised by Picasso (179); and it was familiar to others including Gerald Murphy. See Fitzgerald's extensive description of "refracting objects"—crystal and broken surfaces—at the scene of Rosemary's hotel room ending book 1 of *Tender Is the Night.* He writes in some detail about their effect on the way we think and feel.

33. Ibid., 194.

34. Kirk Curnutt, "'A Unity Less Conventional but Not Less Serviceable': A Narratological History of *Tender Is the Night,*" in Blazek and Rattray, *Twenty-First-Century Readings of* Tender Is the Night, 121–42.

35. Ibid.

36. Vaill, *Everybody Was So Young,* 347, 439. See Herbert, "Outlandish Proverbs" #524, in *The Works of George Herbert,* 339. See Hays and Wickes, "R. E. M and Gerald Murphy," 15.

37. Martz, *The Poetry of Meditation,* 326–27.

38. Summers, *George Herbert: His Religion and Art,* 24.

39. Knights, "George Herbert: Resolution and Conflict," in De Cesare, *George Herbert and the Seventeenth-Century Religious Poets,* 243–44.

40. Ibid., 243. See photographs and text in Vaill, *Everybody Was So Young,* 118–19, 126, for a sense of the importance that Gerald Murphy (and Picasso) ascribed to his appearance.

41. Herbert, *The Works of George Herbert,* 239–43.

42. Gordon, *T. S. Eliot: An Imperfect Life,* 523.

43. Bruccoli, *Some Sort of Epic Grandeur,* 200. Fitzgerald's remarks ap-

peared in *The Crack-Up* in 1936. Bruccoli applies them circa 1924 when Fitzgerald was at Antibes and saw the Murphys regularly.

44. Archibald MacLeish, "Foreword," in Rubin, *The Paintings of Gerald Murphy*, 7–8.

45. Miller, *Letters from the Lost Generation*, 13–14.

46. Miller, "Gerald Murphy in Letters, Literature, and Life," in *Making It New*, ed. Rothschild, 148.

47. MacLeish, in *Reflections*, ed. Drabeck and Ellis, 57.

48. Miller, *Letters from the Lost Generation*, 138–39.

49. Chan and Figura, "The Language of the Body," in Elderfield, Reed, Chan, and González, eds., *ModernStarts: People, Places, Things*, 50. Emphasis added.

50. Miller, *Letters from the Lost Generation*, 163.

51. Whitehead, *Science and the Modern World*, 86. Emphasis added.

52. Ibid., 93–94.

53. Russell, "Styles in Ethics," in *The Basic Writings of Bertrand Russell*, ed. Egner and Denonn, 350.

54. Dewey, "The Metaphysics of Experience," in *The Philosophy of John Dewey*, ed. McDermott, 312.

55. Curnutt, *The Cambridge Introduction to F. Scott Fitzgerald*, 32–33.

56. Miller, *Letters from the Lost Generation*, 87.

57. See Michael K. Glenday, "American Riviera: Style and Expatriation in *Tender Is the Night*," in Blazek and Rattray, *Twenty-First-Century Readings of Tender Is the Night*, 147: at Villa Diana, "leisure and conviviality transcend themselves to approach an ultimate civility of human relationship."

58. Alan Margolies, "Climbing 'Jacob's Ladder,'" in Bryer, *New Essays on F. Scott Fitzgerald's Neglected Stories*, 91–92.

59. Fitzgerald, *The Short Stories of F. Scott Fitzgerald*, ed. Bruccoli, 357–58. See Miller, *Letters from the Lost Generation*, 28: To be momentarily connected "to the universe" was Gerald Murphy's highest praise for Hemingway—and, rarely, for himself.

60. Miller, *Letters from the Lost Generation*, 19, 23, 62, 87, 161.

61. Ibid., 208.

62. Fitzgerald, *The Basil and Josephine Stories*, ed. Bryer and Kuehl, 20. Richard Schickel's *D. W. Griffith: An American Life* argues that the Biograph films are focused on depictions of "the passing moment." These allowed not only poets and novelists but also directors to find the meanings of duration (121).

63. Freud, "The Ego and the Id," in *The Freud Reader*, ed. Gay, 643–44.

64. Kirk Curnutt, "'A Unity Less Conventional but Not Less Serviceable': A Narratological History of *Tender Is the Night*," in Blazek and Rattray, *Twenty-First-Century Readings of* Tender Is the Night, 138. Emphasis in the text.

65. Freud, "The Ego and the Id," in *The Freud Reader*, ed. Gay, 643.

66. Fitzgerald, *The Short Stories of F. Scott Fitzgerald*, ed. Bruccoli, 453, 457.

67. Fitzgerald, "How to Waste Material," in *My Lost City*, ed. West, 79.

Bibliography

Adler, Betty. *H. L. M.: Mencken Bibliography*. Baltimore: Enoch Pratt Free Library, 1971.

Bak, Hans. *Malcolm Cowley: The Formative Years*. Athens: University of Georgia Press, 1993.

Berman, Ronald. *Fitzgerald, Hemingway, and the Twenties*. Tuscaloosa: The University of Alabama Press, 2001.

———. *Fitzgerald-Wilson-Hemingway*. Tuscaloosa: The University of Alabama Press, 2003.

———. *The Great Gatsby and Modern Times*. Urbana: University of Illinois Press, 1996.

———. *Modernity and Progress*. Tuscaloosa: The University of Alabama Press, 2005.

———. *Translating Modernism: Fitzgerald and Hemingway*. Tuscaloosa: The University of Alabama Press, 2009.

Bishop, John Peale, and Edmund Wilson Jr. *The Undertaker's Garland*. New York: Alfred A. Knopf, 1922.

Blazek, William, and Laura Rattray, eds. *Twenty-First-Century Readings of* Tender Is the Night. Liverpool: Liverpool University Press, 2007.

Bost, Pierre. *Photographies modernes*. Paris: Librairie des arts décoratifs, 1928.

Bradbury, Malcolm, and James McFarlane, eds. *Modernism, 1890–1930*. Atlantic Highlands, NJ: Humanities Press, 1978.

Bruccoli, Matthew J. *Classes on F. Scott Fitzgerald*. Columbia: Thomas Cooper Library, University of South Carolina Press, 2001,

———. *Some Sort of Epic Grandeur: The Life of F. Scott Fitzgerald*. Columbia: University of South Carolina Press, 2002.

Bruccoli, Matthew, ed. *New Essays on* The Great Gatsby. Cambridge: Cambridge University Press, 1985.

Bruccoli, Matthew, Scottie Fitzgerald Smith, and Joan P. Kerr, eds. *The Romantic Egoists*. New York: Charles Scribner's Sons, 1974.

Bryer, Jackson R., ed. *New Essays on F. Scott Fitzgerald's Neglected Stories.* Columbia: University of Missouri Press, 1996.

Bryer, Jackson R., Alan Margolies, and Ruth Prigozy, eds. *F. Scott Fitzgerald: New Perspectives.* Athens: University of Georgia Press, 2000.

Bryer, Jackson R., Ruth Prigozy, and Milton R. Stern, eds. *F. Scott Fitzgerald in the Twenty-First Century.* Tuscaloosa: The University of Alabama Press, 2003.

Carr, Virginia Spencer. *Dos Passos: A Life.* New York: Doubleday, 1984.

Cerasulo, Tom. *Authors Out Here: Fitzgerald, West, Parker, and Schulberg in Hollywood.* Columbia: University of South Carolina Press, 2010.

Chan, Mary, and Starr Figura, "The Language of the Body." In *ModernStarts: People, Places, Things,* edited by John Elderfield, Peter Reed, Mary Chan, and Maria del Carmen González, 48–55. New York: Museum of Modern Art, 1999.

Chan, Mary, and Maria del Carmen González, "Modern Places: The Country and the City." In *ModernStarts: People, Places, Things,* edited by John Elderfield, Peter Reed, Mary Chan, and Maria del Carmen González, 171–79. New York: Museum of Modern Art, 1999.

Chatelain, Jean, and Thomas Hoving. *Impressionism: A Centenary Exhibition.* New York: Metropolitan Museum of Art, 1974.

Corrigan, Robert W. *Comedy: Meaning and Form.* San Francisco: Chandler, 1965.

Craig-Martin, Michael. *A Retrospective, 1968–1989.* London: Whitechapel Art Gallery, 1989.

Curnutt, Kirk. *The Cambridge Introduction to F. Scott Fitzgerald.* Cambridge: Cambridge University Press, 2007.

Dabney, Lewis. *Edmund Wilson: A Life in Literature.* New York: Farrar, Straus and Giroux, 2005.

Dabney, Lewis, ed. *Edmund Wilson: Centennial Reflections.* Princeton, NJ: Princeton University Press, 1997.

Daix, Pierre. *Picasso: Life and Art.* New York: HarperCollins, 1993.

Davidson, Donald. *Subjective, Intersubjective, Objective.* Oxford: Clarendon Press, 2001.

Dewey, John. "The Metaphysics of Experience." In *The Philosophy of John Dewey,* edited by John J. McDermott. Chicago: University of Chicago Press, 1981.

Di Cesare, Mario A., ed. *George Herbert and the Seventeenth-Century Religious Poets.* New York: Norton, 1978.

Donaldson, Scott. *Archibald MacLeish: An American Life.* Boston: Houghton Mifflin, 1992.

———. *Fitzgerald and Hemingway: Works and Days.* New York: Columbia University Press, 2009.

Elderfield, John, Peter Reed, Mary Chan, and Maria del Carmen González, eds. *ModernStarts: People, Places, Things.* New York: Museum of Modern Art, 1999.

Eliot, T. S. *Collected Poems, 1909–1962.* New York: Harcourt Brace and World, 1970.

———. *Selected Essays.* New York: Harcourt Brace, 1950.

Fitzgerald, F. Scott. *The Basil and Josephine Stories.* Edited by Jackson R. Bryer and John Kuehl. New York: Collier Macmillan, 1973.

———. *The Beautiful and Damned.* New York: C. Scribner's Sons, 1922.

———. *Before Gatsby: The First Twenty-Six Stories.* Edited by Matthew J. Bruccoli with the assistance of Judith S. Baughman. Columbia: University of South Carolina Press, 2001.

———. *Conversations with F. Scott Fitzgerald.* Edited by Matthew J. Bruccoli and Judith S. Baughman. Jackson: University Press of Mississippi, 2004.

———. *Correspondence of F. Scott Fitzgerald.* Edited by Matthew J. Bruccoli and Margaret M. Duggan. New York: Random House, 1980.

———. *F. Scott Fitzgerald on Authorship.* Edited by Matthew J. Bruccoli, with Judith S. Baughman. Columbia: University of South Carolina Press, 1996.

———. *The Great Gatsby.* Edited by Matthew J. Bruccoli. Cambridge: Cambridge University Press, 1991.

———. *A Life in Letters.* Edited by Matthew J. Bruccoli. New York: Simon and Schuster, 1995.

———. *My Lost City: Personal Essays, 1920–1940.* Edited by James L. W. West III. Cambridge: Cambridge University Press, 2005.

———. *The Pat Hobby Stories.* New York: Collier Macmillan, 1988.

———. *The Price Was High: The Last Uncollected Stories of F. Scott Fitzgerald.* Edited by Matthew J. Bruccoli. New York: Harcourt Brace Jovanovich, 1979.

———. *The Short Stories of F. Scott Fitzgerald.* Edited by Matthew J. Bruccoli. New York: Charles Scribner's Sons, 1989.

———. *Tender Is the Night.* New York: Scribner, 1982.

———. *This Side of Paradise.* Edited by James L. W. West III. Cambridge: Cambridge University Press, 1995.

The F. Scott Fitzgerald Review. 2002. The F. Scott Fitzgerald Society.

Foresta, Merry A., ed. *Perpetual Motif: The Art of Man Ray.* New York: Abbeville Press, 1988.

Freud, Sigmund. *Civilization and Its Discontents.* Edited by James Strachey. New York: Norton, 1989.

———. *The Freud Reader.* Edited by Peter Gay. New York: W. W. Norton, 1989.

Gordon, Lyndall. *T. S. Eliot: An Imperfect Life.* New York: W. W. Norton, 1998.

Graham, Sheilah. *Beloved Infidel: The Education of a Woman.* New York: Henry Holt, 1958.

Graham, T. Austin. "Fitzgerald's 'Riotous Mystery': *This Side of Paradise* as Musical Theater." *The F. Scott Fitzgerald Review* 6 (2007–8): 21–51.

Groom, Winston. *Vicksburg, 1863.* New York: Alfred A. Knopf, 2009.

Hays, Peter, and George Wickes. "R. E. M and Gerald Murphy." *The F. Scott Fitzgerald Society Newsletter* 18 (December 2008): 15.

Hemingway, Ernest. *Death in the Afternoon.* New York: Charles Scribner's Sons, 1960.

———. *The Sun Also Rises.* New York: Scribner, 1954.

Herbert, George. *The Works of George Herbert.* Edited by F. E. Hutchinson. Oxford: Clarendon Press, 1941.

Herbert, Robert L. "Impressionism, Originality, and Laissez-Faire." In *Critical Readings in Impressionism and Post-Impressionism,* edited by Mary Tompkins Lewis, 23-29. Berkeley: University of California Press, 2007.

Hobson, Fred. *Mencken: A Life.* New York: Random House, 1994.

———. *Serpent in Eden: H. L. Mencken and the South.* Baton Rouge: Louisiana State University Press, 1974.

Huysmans, J. K. Untitled reprint from *La réforme,* July 1, 1880. In Jean Chatelain and Thomas Hoving, *Impressionism: A Centenary Exhibition,* 127–29. New York: Metropolitan Museum of Art, 1974.

James, William. *The Philosophy of William James.* New York: Modern Library, 1925.

Knights, L. C. "George Herbert: Resolution and Conflict." In *George Herbert and the Seventeenth-Century Religious Poets,* edited by Mario A Di Cesare, 242–49. New York: Norton, 1978.

Lathbury, Roger. *Literary Masterpieces.* Vol. 1, *The Great Gatsby.* Farmington Hills, MI: Gale, 2000.

Lewis, Mary Tompkins, ed. *Critical Readings in Impressionism and Post-Impressionism.* Berkeley: University of California Press, 2007.

Lewis, Sinclair. *Arrowsmith; Elmer Gantry; Dodsworth.* New York: Library of America, 2002.

Lippmann, Walter. *Public Opinion.* New York: Free Press, 1997.

———. *Public Persons.* Edited by Gilbert A. Harrison. New York: Liveright, 1976.

Lynn, Kenneth S. *Charlie Chaplin and His Times.* New York: Simon and Schuster, 1997.

MacLeish, Archibald. "Foreword." In William Rubin, *The Paintings of Gerald Murphy*, 7–8. New York: Museum of Modern Art, 1974.

———. *Reflections*. Edited by Bernard A. Drabeck and Helen E. Ellis. Amherst: University of Massachusetts Press, 1986.

Man Ray. *Man Ray: Photographs*. London: Thames and Hudson, 1982.

Martz, Louis. *The Poetry of Meditation*. New Haven, CT: Yale University Press, 1954.

Mellow, James R. *Invented Lives: F. Scott and Zelda Fitzgerald*. Boston: Houghton Mifflin, 1984.

Mencken, H. L. *The American Language*. New York: Alfred A. Knopf, 2000.

———. *H. L. Mencken's Smart Set Criticism*. Edited by William H. Nolte. Washington, DC: Gateway, 1987.

———. *A Mencken Chrestomathy*. New York: Alfred A. Knopf, 1967.

———. *Minority Report: H. L. Mencken's Notebooks*. Baltimore: Johns Hopkins University Press, 1997.

———. *My Life as Author and Editor*. New York: Alfred A. Knopf, 1993.

———. *Notes on Democracy*. Edited by Marion Elizabeth Rodgers. New York: Dissident Books, 2009.

———. *Prejudices: First Series*. New York: Knopf, 1919.

———. *Prejudices: Second Series*. London: Jonathan Cape, 1921.

———. *A Second Mencken Chrestomathy*. Edited by Terry Teachout. New York: Alfred A. Knopf, 1995.

Miller, Linda Patterson. "Gerald Murphy in Letters, Literature, and Life." In *Making It New: The Art and Style of Sara and Gerald Murphy*, edited by Deborah Rothschild, 143–63. Berkeley: University of California Press, 2007.

———. *Letters from the Lost Generation*. New Brunswick, NJ: Rutgers University Press, 1991.

Myers, Gerald E. *William James: His Life and Thought*. New Haven, CT: Yale University Press, 1986.

O'Meara, Lauraleigh. *Lost City: Fitzgerald's New York*. New York: Routledge, 2002.

Overy, Richard; *The Morbid Age: Britain between the Wars*. London: Allen Lane and Penguin Books, 2009.

Petry, Alice Hall. *Fitzgerald's Craft of Short Fiction*. Tuscaloosa: The University of Alabama Press, 1989.

Picasso, Pablo. *Pablo Picasso, 1881–1973*. Edited by Ingo F. Walther. Cologne: Taschen, 2006.

Prigozy, Ruth. "Fitzgerald's Flappers and Flapper Films of the Jazz Age: Behind the Morality." In *A Historical Guide to F. Scott Fitzgerald,* edited by Kirk Curnutt, 129–61. Oxford: Oxford University Press, 2004.

———. "From Griffith's Girls to *Daddy's Girl*: The Masks of Innocence in *Tender Is the Night.*" *Twentieth-Century Literature* 26 (Summer 1980): 189–221.

———. *F. Scott Fitzgerald.* London: Penguin, 2001.

———. "'Poor Butterfly': F. Scott Fitzgerald and Popular Music." *Prospects* 2 (1976): 40–67.

Reed, Peter. "Common and Uncommon Things." In *ModernStarts: People, Places, Things,* edited by John Elderfield, Peter Reed, Mary Chan, and Maria del Carmen González, 297–307. New York: Museum of Modern Art, 1999.

Richardson, John. *A Life of Picasso: The Triumphant Years, 1917–1932.* New York: Alfred A. Knopf, 2007.

Rothschild, Deborah, ed. *Making It New: The Art and Style of Sara and Gerald Murphy.* Berkeley: University of California Press, 2007.

———. "Masters of the Art of Living." In *Making It New,* 11–87.

Rubin, William. *The Paintings of Gerald Murphy.* New York: Museum of Modern Art, 1974.

Russell, Bertrand. "Styles in Ethics," In *The Basic Writings of Bertrand Russell,* edited by Robert E. Enger and Lester E. Denonn, 345–50. London: Routledge, 2003.

Ryan, Alan. *John Dewey and the High Tide of American Liberalism.* New York: W. W. Norton, 1997.

Santayana, George. *Character and Opinion in the United States.* Garden City, NY: Doubleday, 1956. Originally published 1920.

———. *The Essential Santayana: Selected Writings.* Bloomington: Indiana University Press, 2009.

———. *The Genteel Tradition: Nine Essays by George Santayana.* Edited by Douglas L. Wilson. Lincoln: University of Nebraska Press, 1998.

Schickel, Richard. *D. W. Griffith: An American Life.* New York: Simon and Schuster, 1984.

Seldes, Gilbert. *The Seven Lively Arts.* New York: Sagamore Press, 1957.

Sklar, Robert. *F. Scott Fitzgerald: The Last Laocoön.* London: Oxford University Press, 1967.

Snyder, Robert W. *The Voice of the City.* Chicago: Ivan R. Dee, 2000.

Sontag, Susan. *On Photography.* New York: Dell, 1977.

Stenerson, Douglas C. *H. L. Mencken: Iconoclast from Baltimore.* Chicago: University of Chicago Press, 1971.

Stoneback, H. R. *Reading Hemingway's* The Sun Also Rises. Kent, OH: Kent State University Press, 2007.

Summers, Joseph. *George Herbert: His Religion and Art.* Cambridge, MA: Harvard University Press, 1954.

Teachout, Terry. *The Skeptic: A Life of H. L. Mencken.* New York: HarperCollins, 2002.

Thomson, Belinda. *Impressionism: Origins, Practice, Reception.* London: Thames and Hudson, 2000.

Trilling, Lionel. *A Gathering of Fugitives.* Boston: Beacon Press, 1956.

———. *The Moral Obligation to Be Intelligent.* Edited by Leon Wieseltier. New York: Farrar, Straus and Giroux, 2000.

Turnbull, Andrew. *Scott Fitzgerald.* New York: Charles Scribner's Sons, 1962.

Vaill, Amanda. *Everybody Was So Young.* Boston: Houghton Mifflin, 1998.

Whitehead, Alfred North. *Science and the Modern World.* New York: Macmillan, 1953.

Williams, William H. A. *H. L. Mencken Revisited.* New York: Twayne, 1998.

Wilson, Edmund. *The American Earthquake.* New York: Da Capo, 1996.

———. *Edmund Wilson: The Man in Letters.* Edited by David Castronovo and Janet Groth. Athens: Ohio University Press, 2001.

———. *From the Uncollected Edmund Wilson.* Edited by Janet Groth and David Castronovo. Athens: Ohio University Press, 1995.

———. *Letters on Literature and Politics, 1912–1972.* Edited by Elena Wilson. New York: Farrar, Straus and Giroux, 1977.

———. *Literary Essays and Reviews of the 1920s & 30s.* Edited by Lewis M. Dabney. New York: Library of America, 2007.

———. *Literary Essays and Reviews of the 1930s & 40s.* Edited by Lewis M. Dabney. New York: Library of America, 2007.

———. *The Twenties.* Edited by Leon Edel. New York: Farrar, Straus and Giroux, 1975.

———. *Upstate.* New York: Farrar, Straus and Giroux, 1971.

Winkfield, Trevor. "The Notebook as Sketchbook." In *Making It New: The Art and Style of Sara and Gerald Murphy,* edited by Deborah Rothschild, 133–41. Berkeley: University of California Press, 2007.

Wittgenstein, Ludwig. *Culture and Value.* Edited by G. H. Von Wright and Heikki Nyman. Chicago: University of Chicago Press, 1980.

———. *The Wittgenstein Reader.* Edited by Anthony Kenny. Oxford: Blackwell, 1994.

Wood, Gordon S. *Empire of Liberty: A History of the Early Republic, 1789–1815.* Oxford: Oxford University Press, 2009.

Index